C000121716

Extreme Practice
For National 5 Maths

EXTREME PRACTICE TEAM

Published 2017

ii

Publication ©InfoStream Media and Publishing Ltd

Cover image ©Getty Images reproduced under license

This book is copyright under the Designs, Patents and Copyright Act of 1988. All rights reserved. Aside from allowable uses under UK copyright legislation, no part of this publication may be reproduced, stored in a retrieval system or transmitted by any means - including but not limited to electronic distribution or photocopying - without prior written permission or under license from InfoStream Media and Publishing Ltd.

A legal deposit copy of this title is available from the British Library.

1st Edition
Printed in the United Kingdom

10 9 8 7 6 5 4 3 2 1

Contents

Preface

"I don't know what's the matter with people: they don't learn by understanding; they learn by some other way—by rote, or something. Their knowledge is so fragile!"
    – Richard P. Feynman, Nobel Laureate, *Surely You're Joking, Mr. Feynman! Adventures of a Curious Character*

Although it sounds absurd to say, problems are the solution to your problem. Your problem is that you need to pass (or hopefully get a very good grade in) National 5 Maths. The reality as shown in the scientific literature is that solving problems is an extremely effective way to learn. This is especially true of mathematics. Read the quote from the great Richard Feynman. Read it again. Understand what it means and apply it to your studies.

Mathematics is not a subject that can simply be memorised. You can read the textbook all day and it will not be very much help. If you do not understand what you are doing you will not do well. If you want to excel in your maths exam you need to do maths not just learn maths. Maths is a practical subject. If you do lots of practice you will do well. For example most people memorise formulae however those who are going to do well do not need to. They have done so much work that the formulae are obvious. If for example you can't remember this equation, you are very likely to fail your exam:

$$a^2 + b^2 = c^2$$

Controversially some of the questions in this book will be above National 5 Maths standard in terms of difficulty but can be done using only National 5 Maths skills. I will mark these with a star after the question number. There is however nothing in this book that is unfair. Every question can be done using only what is in the course or included in the question.

I expect that most students will find this book tough but fair. This is quite deliberate. However there are fully worked solutions for every question in which I show every single step in every single calculation. I will also combine several skills into one question which will make the question much harder if you have any weaknesses in your knowledge. Again, this is deliberate. For example a question on factorising could make you work with fractions, surds, algebra and power laws. If you are good at 4 out of 5 of those things you will get the question wrong. Typically (going by past papers) in the exam you will be asked about one or perhaps two things at a time. To do well in the exam you need to be good at everything. If you go into an exam uncertain of a few sections you are putting your A at risk. By mixing up the questions a little it will expose gaps in your knowledge. If there is one section that you are not good at I will repeatedly punish you for it until you sort it out.

Consider, for example, a student that knows 80% of the course perfectly but can't do 20% at all. Most years this student is likely to get an A or at worst a good B. However random chance comes into play. Imagine for example that one year the paper has 40% of its questions based on the 20% the student can't do - this is completely possible. Under this scenario the student needs to score 100% on the questions he/she can do in order to get a B. If they drop a single mark they will get a C. Do not tolerate gaps in your knowledge. Do the stuff you hate.

I have also been crafty in writing questions. I will often set out to catch you out. I will ask question on what students consistently get wrong or don't learn properly. For example a good B student at National 5 will be able to work with square roots quite well. However give them a cube root and they go to pieces. In this book I will give you the cube root and expose how poor your knowledge of power laws really is.

However, do not be discouraged by getting questions wrong. If you do an hour of study and get nothing wrong you have not learned anything. Your time has been completely wasted. If you get a question totally wrong work with the solution, your notes and, if needed, your teacher until you understand it.

Then use spaced repetition. This is an extremely effective study technique. Do some maths study, get some questions wrong, figure out how to do the questions properly, study another subject and then come back and try them again. Repeat this process until you are getting everything in this book correct without looking at the solutions.

It is also very important to make it completely clear that this book is not official in any sense - for example the SQA has not endorsed it. Although I expect that this book will be hugely helpful and is the book that I wish I had when I was in your shoes; it should not be your only revision material. The BrightRed guides are exceptionally good and are a must. As are past papers and model papers. The questions in this book are not from past papers (they are original) and are not practice exams. The book is not a series of practice exams. It is a huge collection of questions covering the mathematics contained in National 5 Maths with exceptionally detailed solutions. You must do the past papers from the SQA as I don't write the exam, they do.

To conclude this introduction I will leave you with a quote from a review of a competitors book which summed up the philosophy behind this book perfectly:

Dreadful book!
Q- What use is a maths book with no answers?
A - no use at all.

– Customer review, *Amazon UK*

Equations

Not all of these equations will be given in the exam. A good student who has done enough revision will have done so much practice that they will not need an equation sheet. You should aim to not require this sheet.

Quadratic formula:

$$x = \frac{-b \pm \sqrt{b^2 - 4ac}}{2a}$$

Sine Rule:

$$\frac{a}{sin(A)} = \frac{b}{sin(B)} = \frac{c}{sin(C)}$$

Cosine Rule:

$$a^2 = b^2 + c^2 - 2bc cos(A)$$

Volume of a cone:

$$V = \frac{1}{3}\pi R^2 h$$

Volume of a sphere:

$$V = \frac{4}{3}\pi R^3$$

Volume of a pyramid:

$$V = \frac{lwh}{3}$$

Standard Deviation:

$$\sigma = \sqrt{\frac{\sum (X - \overline{X})^2}{N - 1}}$$

Mean (average):

$$\overline{X} = \frac{\sum X}{N}$$

Area of a triangle:

$$A = \frac{1}{2}ab\sin(C)$$

Area of a sector:

$$A = \pi R^2 \times \frac{\theta}{360}$$

Length of an arc:

$$L = 2\pi R \times \frac{\theta}{360}$$

Pythagoras Theorem:

$$a^2 + b^2 = c^2$$

Trigonometry:

$$\cos(\theta) = \frac{A}{H}$$

$$\sin(\theta) = \frac{O}{H}$$

$$\tan(\theta) = \frac{O}{A}$$

Equation of a line:

$$y - b = m(x - a)$$

$$y = mx + c$$

Gradient of a line:

$$m = \frac{y_2 - y_1}{x_2 - x_1}$$

Discriminant:

$$b^2 - 4ac$$

Compound interest/growth formula:

$$V_{final} = V_{initial} \times growth^{years}$$

Exact values of trigonometric functions:

	0°	30°	45°	60°	90°
Sine	0	$\frac{1}{2}$	$\frac{1}{\sqrt{2}}$	$\frac{\sqrt{3}}{2}$	1
Cosine	1	$\frac{\sqrt{3}}{2}$	$\frac{1}{\sqrt{2}}$	$\frac{1}{2}$	0
Tangent	0	$\frac{\sqrt{3}}{2}$	1	$\sqrt{3}$	∞

Hint: if you memorise sine you can get cosine very easily by reflecting about 45°

1

Expressions and Formulae

"To those who do not know mathematics it is difficult to get across a real feeling as to the beauty, the deepest beauty, of nature. ... If you want to learn about nature, to appreciate nature, it is necessary to understand the language that she speaks in"
— Richard P. Feynman, Nobel Laureate, *The Character of Physical Law Lecture, 1964*

1.1. Use your knowledge of index laws to simplify the following expressions writing your answer in the form x^n each time:

$$\text{(a) } \frac{x^2}{x^3} \quad \text{(b) } x^{1/3} \times x^{1/3} \quad \text{(c) } (xy)^2 \times y^2 x$$

1.2. By inspection state the value of a, b, c and d.

$$\sqrt{x} = x^a$$
$$\sqrt[3]{y} = y^b$$
$$\sqrt[6]{y^2} = y^{c/d}$$

1.3. Write the following with a rational denominator.

$$\text{(a) } \frac{3}{\sqrt{2}} \quad \text{(b) } \frac{5}{3\sqrt{2}} \quad \text{(c) } \frac{3}{\sqrt{9}}$$

1.4. Prove the following. Hint: start with the expression on the left and show that it is the same as the expression on the right.

$$\frac{n}{\sqrt{n}} = \frac{n^{\frac{3}{2}}}{n}$$

1.5. Expand the following brackets:

$$\text{(a) } (x+5)(x+1) \quad \text{(b) } (x+3)^2 \quad \text{(c) } \frac{(x+1)(x-3)^3}{(x-3)^2}$$

1.6. Expand the brackets fully and gather like terms:

$$(x + 2)^2(x - 1)$$

1.7. Fully expand the following expression and gather like terms:

$$x(x + 4)^2 + x$$

1.8. Factorise the following expressions using an appropriate method:

(a) $x^2 - 81$ (b) $7x^2 + 4x - 112 - 4x$ (c) $x^2 + 7x + 12$

(d) $6x^2 - 13x - 5$ (e) $6x^2 + 4x - 2$ (f) $\frac{12x^3 - x^2 - 6x}{x}$

1.9. Factorise the following expression using trinomials and common factors:

$$5x^2y + 20xy - 25y$$

1.10.* Apply your knowledge of powers, surds and common factors to factorise the following expression:

$$p^{\frac{5}{2}} + 4p^{\frac{3}{2}} + 3\sqrt{p} = 0$$

Hence find the three solutions to the equation. Note that p may be negative. The solution must therefore be obtained from the factors. Trial and error will not work.

1.11. Multiply out the brackets and factorise the result:

$$5(x + 1)(x + 3) - 3x^2 - 16x - 21$$

1.12. A straight line passes through the points (2,2) and (1,4). Find the gradient.

1.13. A helicopter blade has a radius of 5.7m and the tip path plane is the area swept out when a rotor blade rotates through 360 degrees. The blades follow a circular path when they rotate. There is very complex physics involved in understanding how the rotor blades behave in flight. A designer is looking at what happens between 37 degrees and 64 degrees. Calculate (i) the distance travelled by the blade around the arc of the circle, (ii) the area of the sector of the tip path plane swept out by the blade between these points and (iii) the area of the tip path plane (hint: the area of a circle).

1.14 When asked what the largest pyramid in the world is most people would say the Great Pyramid of Gizza. However the Shard in London (which is almost a pyramid) is much taller. We can approximate the shard as a pyramid with a square base of 55m and a height of 306m. The great Pyramid of Gizza is 139m tall and has a square base of 230m. Which has the largest volume? How many times larger is one than the other?

1.15 We have a cone and a sphere. The radius of the sphere is equal to the radius of the base of the cone. The cone has a height equal to its radius. Which of the two shapes always has the greatest volume regardless of the value of the radius? How much larger is the bigger one than the smaller one?

1.16 Perform the following calculation and express your answer as a surd.

$$x^{-2} \times x^{1.5}$$

1.17. Find the value of a:

$$\sqrt{8} = a\sqrt{a}$$

1.18 A cube has a length and breadth of $\sqrt{2}$ and has a height of $\sqrt{32}$. Find (i) the volume of the cube expressing the surd in its most reduced form and (ii) the total volume of the cube with an extension of volume $\sqrt{8}$ added.

1.19 Factorise by completing the square expressing your answer in the form $a(x+p)^2 + q$:

$$x^2 + 4x + 3$$

1.20. Express the following using four significant figures:

(a) 1.289535   (b) 0.00449   (c) 7059.89

1.21. Simplify and express the answer in scientific notation:

$$\frac{10000}{5 \times 10^6}$$

1.22. A line passes through two distinct points (x_1, y_1) and (x_2, y_2). It is observed that $x_1 \neq x_2$ and $y_1 = y_2$. From this information deduce the gradient of the line.

1.23. In the following figure the line AD is the diameter of the circle
and point C is the centre of the circle. An isosceles triangle is formed by
connecting the points A, B and C where points A and B are on the circle.
If the diameter of the circle is 10 units find the length of the line AB.

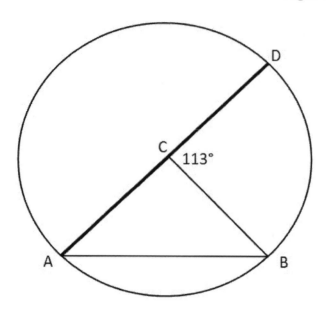

2

Relationships

"I remember once going to see him [Ramanujan] when he was lying ill at Putney. I had ridden in taxi-cab No. 1729, and remarked that the number seemed to be rather a dull one, and that I hoped it was not an unfavourable omen. "No", he replied, "it is a very interesting number; it is the smallest number expressible as the sum of two positive cubes in two different ways"
— G.H. Hardy, *Mathematical Society of America Magazine*

2.1. A line has a gradient of 4 and passes through the point (8,35). Find the equation of this line.

2.2. A design for the middle section of a new ramp is plotted on paper. Find the equation of the line shown in the figure below.

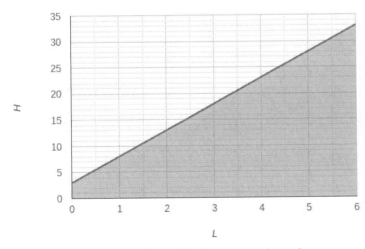

2.3. Two lines are parallel. The lines are plotted on a graph of v against w. The first line has the equation $w = qv + d$. The second line crosses the w axis at a point three units in w below the point where the first line crosses the w-axis. What is the equation of the second line?

2.4. If one line has a gradient of 2 with a y-intercept of 5 and the other has a gradient of 4 and a y-intercept of 10 at what point do these two lines meet?

2.5. If the two lines both had a gradient of 2 but one line has a y-intercept of 5 and the other has a y-intercept of 10 (as before); at what point, if any, do these two lines meet?

2.6. If a line has the equation $y = x$ state what the gradient of the line is. Also determine where this line intersects the line $y = -x$.

2.7.* The relationship between x and y is modeled by line Q. The point (a,b) is on line Q. The line $x = a - 4$ intercepts line Q at $y = b + 1$. What is the gradient of line Q?

2.8. Some equations can be difficult to factorise as the factors are not easy to see. Factorise the following equation:

$$x^2 + 5x + 2 = 0$$

Given that we know it has the solution:

$$x = \frac{1}{2}(\pm\sqrt{17} - 5)$$

2.9. Show that the following equation has only one solution.

$$x^2 + 6x + 9 = 0$$

2.10. Draw a sketch of a shape which has a volume of l^3 and shade in an area equal to l^2

2.11. If a certain shape has a volume given by ldh where h is its height d is its depth and l is its length and none of these dimensions are equal; draw a diagram of the shape and shade the area given by dh.

2.12. Which of the following equations has the highest number of real roots?

$$(x - 2)^3 = 0 \qquad (1)$$
$$x^2 + 5x - 15 = 0 \quad (2)$$
$$3x^2 - 7x + 19 = 0 \quad (3)$$

2.13. The number 1729 in the quote at the start of this section is what is known as a taxicab number in number theory. This number is the smallest number that can be written as the sum of two cubes in two different ways. One way is using 1 and 12 (i.e. $1729 = 1^3 + 12^3$) and another is using 9 and x. By writing an equation for this relationship find x.

2.14. Draw a sketch of the following function between 0 and 6.

$$R = \frac{2(x-3)^4 + \sqrt{2}^2 (x-3)^2}{(x-3)^2}$$

2.15. Find the co-ordinates of the turning point and the equation of the axis of symmetry for a parabola given by the equation $-2(x+1)^2 + 4$. What is the nature of this turning point?

2.16. At what value of x does the lowest value of y occur for a function of equation $y = (x-1)(x-2) - 3$? Hint: start by multiplying out and complete the square.

2.17. A parabola has the equation $y = k(x-a)^2 + b$. If the parabola has a maximum turning point located at (1,-2) and $k = 1$ what is its equation? From the equation sketch the parabola between $x = -2$ and $x = 4$.

2.18. The turning points of two parabolas are connected by a line P. One parabola has equation $y = -(x-2)^2 + 1$ and another has the equation $y = (x-5)^2 + 5$. Find the length of line P. Hint: Pythagoras will help.

2.19. Solve the following system of equations simultaneously:

$$4x + 5y = 19$$
$$2x + 3y = 9$$

2.20. Simultaneous equations can be used to solve the following classic problem. A bat and a ball together cost £1.10. If the bat costs £1 more than the ball how much does the ball cost?

2.21. A bizarre discovery by Albert Einstein is that the time is not constant everywhere and is affected by relative velocity. It was shown by Hafele and Keating that an atomic clock on the earth showed a different time to an atomic clock on an aeroplane which has flown twice around the world. The famous equation governing time dilation is given below. Change the subject of the equation to velocity, V.

$$T' = T\sqrt{1 - \frac{V^2}{c^2}}$$

2.22. Identify the hypotenuse of the following triangle and prove that the following triangle has a right angle.

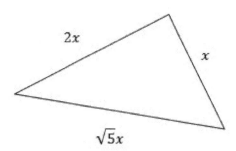

2.23. The following figure shows two cosine graphs. By using a phase angle, ϕ, these graphs can be written in terms of sine. Find the equation of the graph below in the form $y = sin(x + \phi)$.

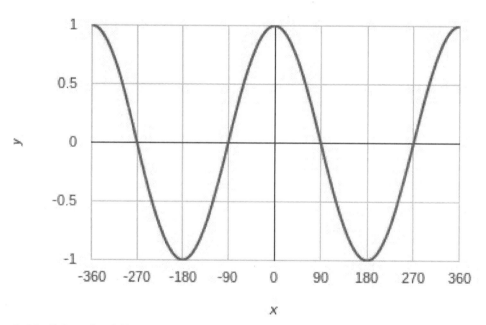

2.24. Solve the following inequation:

$$-4x < -8$$

2.25. Solve the following system of equations graphically:

$$E - 4x = 3$$

$$E - 5x = 1$$

Hint: A sketch between $x = 0$ and $x = 5$ is sufficient.

3

Applications

3.1. Simplify the following fractions showing all steps:

(a) $\frac{1}{2} + \frac{1}{4}$ (b) $\frac{3}{5} - \frac{80}{400}$ (c) $-\frac{5}{2} + \frac{3}{4}$

(d) $\frac{1}{2} \times \frac{1}{2}$ (e) $2 + \frac{7}{19}$ (f) $\frac{6}{7} + 2 \times \frac{0.5}{7}$

(g) $0.7 + \frac{2}{20}$ (h) $\left(\frac{1}{5} + \frac{1}{4}\right) \div \frac{5}{4}$ (i) $\left(\frac{1}{2}\right)^2 + \frac{1}{y} \div \frac{1}{x}$

3.2.* Express the following complex fraction in its simplest form as a standard fraction. Hint: combine the fractions on the top and then combine those at the bottom and then divide the two fractions. Applying basic rules of factions, simple algebra and a sensible order of operation will give the right answer.

$$\frac{\frac{1}{x} + \frac{1}{y}}{\frac{1}{y} - z}$$

3.3 Perform the following multiplication and present your answer with a rational denominator:

$$\frac{5}{2} \times \frac{1}{sin(45)}$$

3.4. An estate agent charges a seller a fee of £3840 to sell her house at a commission rate of 1.5%. How much did the house sell for?

3.5. According to the latest form 10-K filed with the Securities and Exchange Commission, shares in Warren Buffett's Berkshire Hathaway have returned 20.8 % compound between 1965 and 2015. If you had invested £1,000 in Berkshire Hathaway in 1965 what would your shares be worth in 2015 when the 10-K number was calculated? Round your answer to the nearest million.

3.6. If I throw a ball straight up in the air and it reaches a height of x metres.

(i) Write a vector to represent the balls position at the instant that it reaches a height of x metres?

Also if this vector is divided by its magnitude the unit position vector is obtained. Find the unit position vector.

3.7. (i) Find the value of x given that A and B have the same magnitude.

$$A = \begin{pmatrix} x \\ x \\ x \end{pmatrix}$$

$$B = \begin{pmatrix} 3 \\ 0 \\ 3 \end{pmatrix}$$

(ii) Calculate vector C.

$$C = A + 2B$$

(iii) Finally, demonstrate that the magnitude of A is the same as the magnitude of -A.

3.8. A very strange netball team was made up of seven players. Three of the players are 6 years old, two are seven, one is eight and the last player is Jeanne Calment who is 122. Calculate the average age of the team and the standard deviation of the ages. Comment on whether this average is reflective of the team and the size of the standard deviation calculated.

3.9. Using the definitions given find an expression for cotangent (cot) in terms of sine and cosine.

$$tan\theta = \frac{sin\theta}{cos\theta}$$

$$cot\theta = 1 \div tan\theta$$

3.10. Perform the following calculation:

$$2 \begin{pmatrix} 1 \\ 3 \\ 6 \end{pmatrix} + \begin{pmatrix} 4 \\ 2 \\ 1 \end{pmatrix}$$

3.11. The following diagram shows a triangle with a right angle. Find an expression for the length of side S in terms of x as a single fraction in its simplest form.

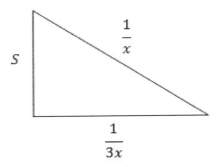

3.12. Find the upper and lower quartiles of the following data. Furthermore calculate the semi-interquartile range.

Data: 1, 4, 7, 2, 8, 2, 16, 4, 5, 8, 9, 2, 5, 4, 6, 7, 1, 4, 5

3.13. Calculate the value of angle A. Hence find the third angle using a basic property of all triangles.

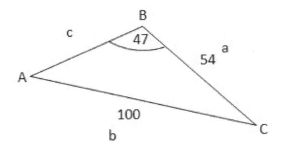

π. Calculate all angles and sides in the following triangle. You must use the cosine rule to find q but may use the sine rule otherwise.

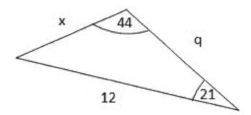

3.15. Find the area of the triangle shown in the previous question.

4

Practice Problems Set 1

4.1. Solve the following inequality and express your answer with x on the left hand side.

$$10 < x + 5$$

4.2. Multiply out the brackets and gather like terms:

$$(x - 2)^2(x + 1)$$

4.3. Perform the following calculation expressing your answer in the form x^n where n is a polynomial.

$$\frac{x^{y+2}}{x^{y^2+2y-8}}$$

4.4. Scientists often express results as a result plus or minus an error i.e. $x \pm \sigma$. In this case x is the mean and σ is the standard deviation. Calculate the mean and standard deviation for experiment 1. Express your final answer in the form $x \pm \sigma$.

Experiment 1: 3 6 7 2 8 9 5 8

4.5. A second experiment was conducted and compared to the experiment in question 4.4. The second experiment yielded an answer of 9 ± 0.4. The scientist concludes that the two experiments produced the same result after taking account of the errors involved. Is this conclusion valid?

If the experiment is based on repeatedly observing the same thing which experiment would you expect to be more reliable?

4.6. If a parabola has a turning point located at (a,b) what is the equation of the parabola's axis of symmetry?

4.7. A line with an equation of the form $y = mx + c$ passes through the point (1,3) and then through the point (3,q). What is the equation of this line in terms of x, y and the unknown q?

4.8. The equation of the subsequent graph can be written as $y = ksin(x+\phi_1)$ or $y = kcos(x + \phi_2)$. Find k, ϕ_1 and ϕ_2.

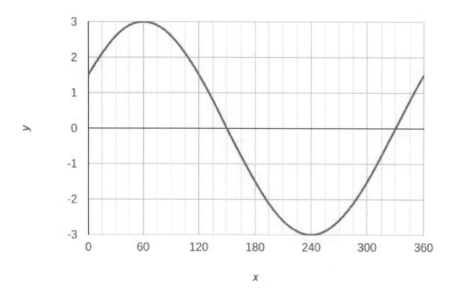

4.9. An investor buys stock in Valeant Pharmaceuticals (NYSE: VRX). The stock price falls 91%. If the investor has £1,170 of VRX stock after the fall what did she invest originally.

4.10. Express 0.0000003 in scientific notation.

4.11. Sketch a graph of $y = 2sin(x + 90)°$.

4.12. Two apples and 5 pears costs £1.90. One apple, four pears and a banana costs £1.80. If a banana costs 40p how much does an apple cost and how much does a pear cost?

4.13. Following an energy crisis energy prices are 21 % higher than last year. If a family paid £650 this year how much did they pay last year assuming they used exactly the same amount of energy?

4.14. Find the magnitude of the vector 4A-0.5B where:

$$A = \begin{pmatrix} 2 \\ 3 \\ 5 \end{pmatrix}$$

$$B = \begin{pmatrix} 2 \\ 6 \\ 8 \end{pmatrix}$$

4.15. A cylinder has a radius of 1.5m and a height of 4m. If the cylinder is 78% full of water what is the volume of water in the cylinder?

4.16. Factorise and solve for x:

$$3x^2 + 3x - 6 = 0$$

4.17. Solve for t:

$$\frac{t}{4} + \frac{15}{8} = 4t$$

5

Practice Problems Set 2

5.1 Calculate and express in four significant figures:

$$\frac{\pi}{272}$$

5.2. What is the gradient and y intercept for a line with the equation given below that passes through the point (-4,-15)?

$$y + 15 = 4x + 18 - 2$$

5.3. Incredibly the period of a pendulum does not depend on its mass. It depends only its length and gravity. Also if you measure the length of a pendulum and time its period you can estimate the value of acceleration due to gravity. Change the subject of the formula to g to facilitate this.

$$T = 2\pi\sqrt{\frac{L}{g}}$$

5.4. By completing the square find the turning point of the parabola given by the equation below and state its nature.

$$y = x^2 + 4x + 8$$

5.5. The diagram below shows a non-right angled triangle. Given that $q = 16$ and that $k = q^{-\frac{1}{2}}$ find the length of the side labeled p.

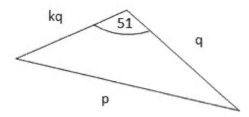

5.6. An investor loses 63% of his investment leaving £3890.92. How much did they invest originally?

5.7. Perform the following calculation and express your answer in the simplest form:

$$(2 \times \frac{2}{8} - \frac{1}{6}) \div \frac{2}{4}$$

5.8.* Multiply out the brackets and gather like terms:

$$(x - (\frac{5}{4} + \frac{\sqrt{89}}{4}))(x + (\frac{\sqrt{89}}{4} - \frac{5}{4})) = 0$$

5.9. How many roots does the following equation have and what is their nature?

$$x^2 + 9x - 2 = 0$$

5.10. A man works for a company that performs very well. He starts work at the company when he is 18 years old and buys £10,000 of the companies stock. The stock performs well and grows at 16% per annum compound. If he never sells stock, never receives a dividend and never buys any more stock what will his investment be worth when he retires at age 70?

5.11. Find the approximate equation of the line of best fit for the following scatter graph:

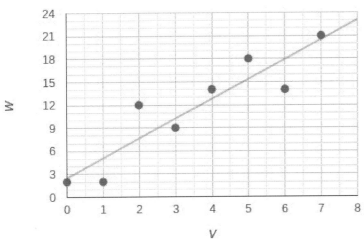

5.12. A triangle has sides of length 3 and 4 and a hypotenuse of length 5. Determine using the converse of Pythagoras whether this triangle has a right angle or not.

5.13. By rationalising the denominator and simplifying or otherwise; show that the following expression can be reduced to the form $\sqrt{a}$ and find the value of a.

$$\frac{9}{\sqrt{27}}$$

5.14. (i) Calculate the mean, standard deviation and semi-interquartile range of the following set of test scores:

6, 4, 8, 4, 6, 8, 12, 2, 4

(ii) A second class has the same mean but a higher standard deviation. What does this imply?

(iii) A third class has the same mean but a lower semi-interquartile range. What does this imply?

5.15. Solve $4x^2 + 2x - 3 = 0$ for x

5.16. State the values of a, b and c in the equation $y = a\cos(bx + c)$ which is shown in the graph below

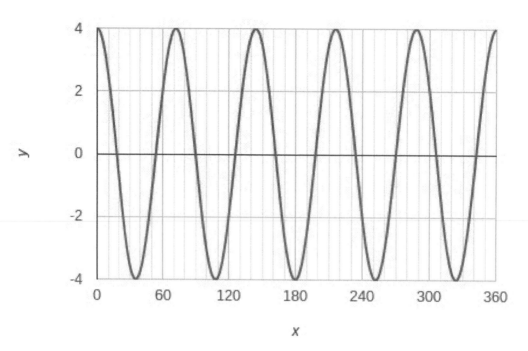

5.17.* A circle has radius R. A segment of the circle has an angle of θ. Express the area of the sector divided by the length of the arc of the segment in terms of the circles radius alone.

5.18.* The following graph does not have any values on its y axis. The parabola has the equation $y = (x-1)^2 + 1$. Find the equation of the line shown:

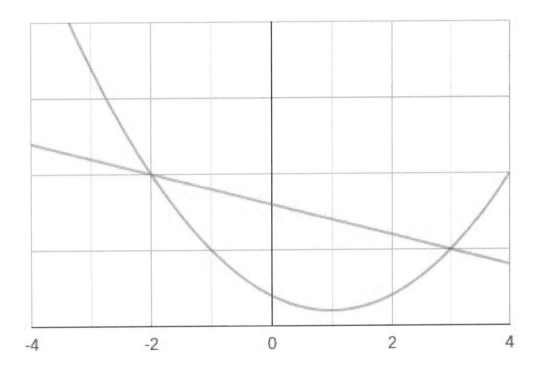

6

Minimum Competency

6.1. Find the mean and standard deviation of the following simple data set:

3, 2, 4, 1

6.2. Perform the following operation:

$$(\frac{2}{3} \div \frac{3}{4}) + \frac{1}{2}$$

6.3. Find vector s and the magnitude of vector s when $s = \frac{1}{4}u + v$ and vectors u and v are given by:

$$u = \begin{pmatrix} 8 \\ -16 \end{pmatrix}$$

$$v = \begin{pmatrix} -9 \\ -6 \end{pmatrix}$$

6.4. If a line passes through the points $(2,10)$ and $(5,19)$ what is the equation of the line?

6.5. Determine the nature of the roots of:

$$x^2 + 6x - 2 = 0$$

6.6. Multiply out the brackets and collect like terms:

$$(x + 2)(x + 5)$$

6.7. What is the co-ordinates of the turning point of a parabola with equation:

$$y = (x + 2)^2 - 5$$

6.8. The graph below shows a parabola. State the nature of the turning point.

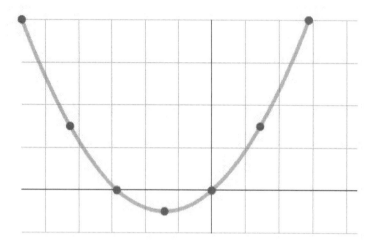

6.9. Factorise the following equation by expressing your answer in the form $(x - a)^2 + b$:

$$x^2 - 6x + 15 = 0$$

6.10. What is the equation of this graph?

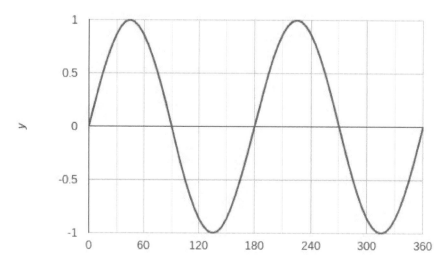

6.11. Express the following with a rational denominator:

$$\frac{3}{\sqrt{6}}$$

6.12. Factorise the following equation by using both a common factor and trinomials:

$$3x^2 + 3x - 60$$

6.13. If a cone has a height of 10cm and a base radius of 4cm what is its volume. Round your answer to two significant figures.

6.14. Rearrange the following equation to make v the subject:

$$W = \frac{1}{2}m(v^2 - u^2)$$

6.15. Use the quadratic formula to solve:

$$2x^2 + 3x - 2 = 0$$

6.16. Rearrange the following equation to make $cosx$ the subject of the equation:

$$cos^2x + sin^2x = 1$$

6.17. Find the area of the triangle shown below:

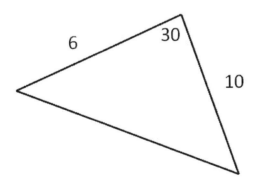

6.18. A saver invests £100 at 0.25% interest compounded annually. After 5 year what will the account balance be?

6.19. In the first half of 2016 the Drax power station in Yorkshire generated $10.9 \times 10^{12}Wh$ where Wh stands for Watt hours. If $1000Wh=1KWh$ how many $KWhs$ did the Drax power plant generate?

6.20. Find the value of g when $x = 2$ where g can be obtained from the following relationships:

$$g = f(x) + 1$$

And

$$f(x) = x^2 + x + 1$$

7

Challenge Problems Set

"Train hard, fight easy"
— Generalissimo Alexander Suvorov, *The Art of Victory*

7.1.* (i) Prove that the following expression is true:

$$\frac{\sqrt{m}}{n} = \frac{m}{n\sqrt{m}}$$

(ii) Using the above equation which you have just proved rewrite the expression below with an irrational denominator:

$$\frac{\sqrt{2}}{3}$$

(iii) Show that when $m = n$ the expression above reduces to:

$$\frac{n}{\sqrt{n}} = \frac{n^{\frac{3}{2}}}{n}$$

(iv) Show that the computation below always results in an irrational denominator when t is a positive integer (i.e. normal numbers like 1,2,3.. and not zero):

$$\frac{\sqrt{m}}{n} \times \left(\frac{\sqrt{n}}{\sqrt{n}}\right)^{2t+1}$$

7.2.* In control theory zeros are the values of s for which $H(s) = 0$ and poles are the values of s for which $H(s) = \infty$ (i.e. infinity). $H(s) = \infty$ when the denominator of $H(s)$ is zero.

(i) Find the poles and zeros of $H(s)$.

$$H(s) = \frac{(s+5)}{(s-1)(s^2 + 3s + 2)}$$

(ii) Find the poles and zeros of $\frac{1}{H(s)}$.

(iii) If you were to plot the value of $H(s)$ between 0 and just before the only positive pole would you expect the gradient of the tangent at point s=q to increase or decrease as you increase q?

7.3.* Two sides of a triangle are given by the vectors A and B as below:

$$A = \begin{pmatrix} 2 \\ 3 \end{pmatrix}$$

$$B = \begin{pmatrix} 1 \\ 2 \end{pmatrix}$$

The third side of the triangle is a line connecting the ends of vectors A and B. The angle between vectors A and B is θ and can be found from the following relationship where A $\cdot$ B (the dot product) is explained subsequently and $|A|$ is the magnitude of vector A.

$$cos(\theta) = \frac{A \cdot B}{|A||B|}$$

Where A and B are column vectors with i rows and j=1 columns the dot product, $A \cdot B$, is the summation of the products of the element in the ith row of A and the element in the ith row of B from i=1 to i. For example the first and last terms in the summation will be $A_1 B_1$ and $A_i B_i$ respectively.

Find the area of the triangle.

7.4.* A car is bought for £10,000 and depreciates 10 % per year for 10 years and then becomes collectible and appreciates 10 % per year for a further 10 years. What is the car worth after 20 years?

7.5.* A physicist reduces a complex problem down to two equations. The system of equations has two solutions for y and three solutions for x. Find all solutions of the system.

$$(y+1)(y-1) = 0$$

$$x^2 - 2xy = -y$$

7.6.* Factorise the following in the form $2(x \pm a)(x \pm b)$.

$$2x^2 - 4x - 2 = 0$$

7.7.* (i) Show that a quadratic equation given by $ax^2 + 2\sqrt{a}\sqrt{c}x + c = 0$ has the solution:

$$x = -\frac{\sqrt{c}}{\sqrt{a}}$$

(ii) Hence solve the equation $4x^2 + 12x + 9 = 0$.

(iii) Show that the equation can always be factorised to $(\sqrt{a}x + \sqrt{c})^2 = 0$ and change the subject of the factorised equation to x to confirm that the solution above is correct.

7.8.* Write with a rational denominator wherein the denominator is raised to a power of one.

$$\frac{y}{\sqrt[3]{x}}$$

7.9.* (i) Find the value of q.

$$x^2 + 81 = (x - 9q)(x + 9q) = 0$$

(ii) Show that this equation has no real solutions.

(iii) Use the value of q you have found to state what the solution to the equation is.

7.10.* Angles can be measured using various scales. Instead of degrees we can use radians. 360 degrees in radians is 2π. If the angle of a sector θ is measured in radians show that the area of this sector is one half of the product of the radius of the circle, R times the length of the arc, L.

8

Fully Worked Solutions

8.1 Expressions and Formulae

1.1. (a) Rule: when dividing you subtract the powers. Hence:

$$\frac{x^2}{x^3} = x^{2-3} = x^{-1} = \frac{1}{x}$$

(b) Rule: when multiplying you add the powers. Hence:

$$x^{1/3} \times x^{1/3} = x^{1/3+1/3} = x^{2/3}$$

This can be simplified. The bottom number is the root and the top is the power on x. Hence:

$$x^{2/3} = \sqrt[3]{x^2}$$

(c) Just add the powers and expand the brackets:

$$(xy)^2 \times y^2 x = x^2 y^2 \times xy^2 = x^{2+1} y^{2+2} = x^3 y^4$$

1.2. The important rule is:

$$\sqrt[z]{x^y} = x^{\frac{y}{z}}$$

Applying this logic we can see that

$$a = \frac{1}{2}$$

$$b = \frac{1}{3}$$

$$c = 2 \text{ and } d = 6$$
$$\text{or } c = 1 \text{ and } d = 3$$

1.3.(a) Rule: Multiply top and bottom by the denominator:

$\frac{3}{\sqrt{2}} = \frac{3}{\sqrt{2}} \times \frac{\sqrt{2}}{\sqrt{2}} = \frac{3\sqrt{2}}{2}$

(b) Multiplying by the whole denominator gives the same answer. Remember that you are just multiplying by one when the top and bottom of the fraction are the same which does not change anything. Hence:

$\frac{5}{3\sqrt{2}} = \frac{5}{3\sqrt{2}} \times \frac{\sqrt{2}}{\sqrt{2}} = \frac{5\sqrt{2}}{6}$

Alternatively:

$\frac{5}{3\sqrt{2}} = \frac{5}{3\sqrt{2}} \times \frac{3\sqrt{2}}{3\sqrt{2}} = \frac{15\sqrt{2}}{18} = \frac{15\sqrt{2} \div 3}{18 \div 3} = \frac{5\sqrt{2}}{6}$

Notice that both answers are the same since:

$\frac{\sqrt{2}}{\sqrt{2}} = \frac{3\sqrt{2}}{3\sqrt{2}} = 1$

(c) Notice that $\sqrt{9} = 3$. Hence:

$$\frac{3}{\sqrt{9}} = \frac{3}{3} = \frac{1}{1} = 1$$

It is also correct to say that:

$$\frac{3}{\sqrt{9}} = \frac{3\sqrt{9}}{9}$$

But notice that this also cancels to 1.

1.4. As stated in the question start with the left hand side and turn it into the right hand side:

$$\frac{n}{\sqrt{n}} = \frac{n}{\sqrt{n}} \times \frac{\sqrt{n}}{\sqrt{n}} = \frac{n\sqrt{n}}{n} = \frac{n \times n^{\frac{1}{2}}}{n} = \frac{n^{1+\frac{1}{2}}}{n} = \frac{n^{\frac{3}{2}}}{n}$$

1.5. (a) $(x+5)(x+1) = x^2 + 5x + x + 5 = x^2 + 6x + 5$

Check by factorising $5 \times 1 = 5$ and $5 + 1 = 6$ so $x^2 + 6x + 5 = (x+5)(x+1)$

(b) $(x+3)^2 = (x+3)(x+3) = x^2 + 3x + 3x + 9 = x^2 + 6x + 9$

Lazy check: $(x+3)(x+3) = 0$ when $x = -3$ and $(-3)^2 + 6(-3) + 9 = 0$

(c) Step 1 use index laws to cancel the $(x-3)$ terms:

$$\frac{(x+1)(x-3)^3}{(x-3)^2} = (x+1)(x-3)$$

Step 2: Expand as usual:

$$(x+1)(x-3) = x^2 + x - 3x - 3 = x^2 - 2x - 3$$

As before at $x = -1$ we have $(-1)^2 - 2(-1) - 3 = 1 + 2 - 3 = 0$

1.6. First take care of the squared term:

$$(x+2)^2 = (x+2)(x+2) = x^2 + 2x + 2x + 4 = x^2 + 4x + 4$$

Hence we can substitute:

$$(x+2)^2(x-1) = (x^2 + 4x + 4)(x-1)$$

Now do the second multiplication:

$$(x^2 + 4x + 4)(x-1) = x^3 - x^2 + 4x^2 - 4x + 4x - 4 = x^3 + 3x^2 - 4$$

1.7. The key is to work logically. Remember BODMAS (do the calculation in the following order: brackets, division, multiplication, addition then subtraction)

Hence we start with the brackets:

$$(x+4)^2 = (x+4)(x+4) = x^2 + 8x + 16$$

Now do the multiplication and addition:

$$x(x^2 + 8x + 16) + x = x^3 + 8x^2 + 16x + x = x^3 + 8x^2 + 17x$$

1.8. (a) This is a difference of two squares since $9^2 = 81$. Hence:

$$x^2 - 81 = (x+9)(x-9)$$

(b) This involves several steps. Firstly the $4x$ terms cancel:

$$7x^2 + 4x - 112 - 4x = 7x^2 - 112$$

Now notice that there is a common factor of 7:

$$7x^2 - 112 = 7(x^2 - 16)$$

Also spot that $16 = 4^2$ so we have a difference of two squares. Hence we can factorise further:

$$7(x^2 - 16) = 7(x + 4)(x - 4)$$

(c) This is a simple trinomial. $12 = 4 \times 3$ and $7 = 3 + 4$. Hence:

$$x^2 + 7x + 12 = (x + 4)(x + 3)$$

(d) This is more tricky. First check for a common factor - there are none. Hence we will have a number in front of x^2. There are two possibilities $6x^2 = 6x \times x$ or $6x^2 = 3x \times 2x$. You can try both of these. $6x^2 = 6x \times x$ won't work. So try $6x^2 = 3x \times 2x$.

$$6x^2 - 13x - 5 = (3x\pm?)(2x\pm?)$$

We need two numbers that multiply to -5. The only possible whole number combinations are 5 and -1 or -5 and 1. We now go through the possible combinations:

$$(3x + 5)(2x - 1)$$
$$(3x - 1)(2x + 5)$$
$$(3x - 5)(2x + 1)$$
$$(3x + 1)(2x - 5)$$

Check which one adds to give the $-13x$ we need. For example the first one does not work.

$$3x \times -1 + 2x \times 5 = -3x + 10x = 7x...nope$$

The last one does however work:

$$3x \times -5 + 2x \times 1 = -13x...correct$$

Therefore the final answer is:

$$6x^2 - 13x - 5 = (3x + 1)(2x - 5)$$

Thankfully this is as tough as trinomials are likely to get.

(e) Always start by looking for a common factor. In this case it is 2.

$$6x^2 + 4x - 2 = 2(3x^2 + 2x - 1)$$

Now do the factorising. It will have to be $3x$ and x.

$$3x^2 + 2x - 1 = (3x \pm ?)(x \pm ?)$$

We need two numbers that multiply to -1 so $1 \times -1 = -1$. In the same way go though the possibilities to find the one that works which is:

$$3x^2 + 2x - 1 = (3x - 1)(x + 1)$$

Putting it back together gives:

$$6x^2 + 4x - 2 = 2(3x - 1)(x + 1)$$

(f) As always check for a common factor first. In this case it is x which cancels.

$$\frac{12x^3 - x^2 - 6x}{x} = \frac{x(12x^2 - x - 6)}{x} = 12x^2 - x - 6$$

Now it is just more practice of the harder trinomials students hate (haha, I get to use Wolfram):

$$12x^2 - x - 6 = (3x + 2)(4x - 3)$$

1.9 As always start by looking for the common factor. Here it is $5y$. Then factorise as usual.

$$5x^2y + 20xy - 25y = 5y(x^2 + 4x - 5) = 5y(x + 5)(x - 1)$$

1.10. In this case we have a common factor of $\sqrt{p}$. We know that $\sqrt{p} = p^{\frac{1}{2}}$.
When we take a factor of $p^{\frac{1}{2}}$ we have to divide through by $p^{\frac{1}{2}}$ which means
subtracting $\frac{1}{2}$ from all the powers.

$$p^{\frac{5}{2}} + 4p^{\frac{3}{2}} + 3\sqrt{p} = \sqrt{p}(p^{\frac{5}{2}-\frac{1}{2}} + 4p^{\frac{3}{2}-\frac{1}{2}} + 3p^{\frac{1}{2}-\frac{1}{2}}) = \sqrt{p}(p^2 + 4p + 3)$$

Now factorise as usual:

$$\sqrt{p}(p^2 + 4p + 3) = \sqrt{p}(p+1)(p+3)$$

The three solutions come from:

$$\sqrt{p} = 0$$
$$p + 1 = 0$$
$$p + 3 = 0$$

Hence the solutions are $p = 0$, $p = -1$ and $p = -3$.

1.11 Work carefully and logically:

$$5(x+1)(x+3) - 3x^2 - 16x - 21$$
$$= 5(x^2 + 4x + 3) - 3x^2 - 16x - 21$$
$$= 5x^2 + 20x + 15 - 3x^2 - 16x - 21$$
$$= 2x^2 + 4x - 6$$

Now factorise. As always start by looking for a common factor:

$$2x^2 + 4x - 6 = 2(x^2 + 2x - 3) = 2(x+3)(x-1)$$

1.12. So $(x_1, y_1) = (1, 4)$ and $(x_2, y_2) = (2, 2)$. So we can get the gradient
from:

$$m = \frac{y_2 - y_1}{x_2 - x_1} = \frac{2 - 4}{2 - 1} = -2$$

A sketch can be used as a common sense check. Does the line go down 2 for
every one we go along?

1.13. (i) For the first part we want the distance travelled between 37 and 64 degrees. We need to use the formula for the arc of a circle:

$$L = 2\pi R \times \frac{\theta}{360}$$

Where:

$$\theta = 64 - 37 = 27 deg$$

Substitute for θ and R to find L:

$$L = 2\pi \times 5.7 \times \frac{27}{360} = 2.69m$$

(ii) Follows on from the last part but uses the equation for the sector area, A:

$$A = \pi R^2 \times \frac{\theta}{360}$$

$$A = \pi \times 5.7^2 \times \frac{27}{360} = 7.66m^2$$

(iii) As the hint says this is just the area of a circle. Hence the area of the tip path plane (tpp):

$$A_{tpp} = \pi \times R^2 = \pi \times 5.7^2 = 102.1m^2$$

1.14. We need to do the calculations which we can do from the equation for the volume of a pyramid.

$$V = \frac{lwh}{3}$$

A square base means that l and w are equal. Now let's start with the Shard:

$$V_{shard} = \frac{lwh}{3} = \frac{55 \times 55 \times 306}{3} = 3.09 \times 10^5$$

Now for the Great Pyramid of Gizza:

$$V_{gizza} = \frac{lwh}{3} = \frac{230 \times 230 \times 139}{3} = 2.45 \times 10^6$$

Hence the great pyramid is bigger. Now find by how much:

$$\frac{V_{gizza}}{V_{shard}} = \frac{2.45 \times 10^6}{3.09 \times 10^5} = 7.93$$

Hence we can say, with rounding, that the Great Pyramid of Gizza is approximately 8 times larger than the Shard in volume.

1.15. Start with the equations:

$$V_{sphere} = \frac{4}{3}\pi R^3_{sphere}$$

$$V_{cone} = \frac{1}{3}\pi R^2_{cone} h_{cone}$$

The question says that the cone and sphere have the same radius which we can call R and that h=R. Hence the equations become:

$$V_{sphere} = \frac{4}{3}\pi R^3$$

$$V_{cone} = \frac{1}{3}\pi R^2 R = \frac{1}{3}\pi R^3$$

Therefore the sphere is always bigger as $\frac{4}{3}$ is greater than $\frac{1}{3}$.

$$\frac{V_{sphere}}{V_{cone}} = \frac{\frac{4}{3}\pi R^3}{\frac{1}{3}\pi R^3} = \frac{\frac{4}{3}}{\frac{1}{3}}$$

Now do the fractions work:

$$\frac{\frac{4}{3}}{\frac{1}{3}} = \frac{4}{3} \div \frac{1}{3} = \frac{4}{3} \times \frac{3}{1} = 4$$

So the sphere is always 4 times larger than this special case cone for every value of R.

1.16. When multiplying powers you add them. Hence:

$$x^{-2} \times x^{1.5} = x^{-2+1.5} = x^{-0.5} = x^{-\frac{1}{2}}$$

You should know by now that the power of one half is the same as a square root. Hence:

$$x^{-\frac{1}{2}} = \frac{1}{\sqrt{x}}$$

1.17. Very simple. We need a square number and non-square number that multiplies to 8. For this 2 and 4 are perfect.

$$\sqrt{8} = \sqrt{4 \times 2} = \sqrt{4}\sqrt{2} = 2\sqrt{2}$$

Therefore $a = 2$

1.18. (i) Very basic maths tells us that the volume of the cube is:

$$V = \sqrt{2} \times \sqrt{2} \times \sqrt{32}$$

We know that $32 = 8 \times 4$ and obviously $\sqrt{2} \times \sqrt{2} = 2$. Hence:

$$2 \times \sqrt{8 \times 4} = 2 \times \sqrt{8} \times \sqrt{4}$$

Just like in 1.17 we can simplify as we know $\sqrt{8} = 2\sqrt{2}$. Thus:

$$2 \times \sqrt{8} \times \sqrt{4} = 2 \times 2\sqrt{2} \times 2 = 8\sqrt{2}$$

(ii) This is simply:

$$8\sqrt{2} + \sqrt{8} = 8\sqrt{2} + 2\sqrt{2} = 10\sqrt{2}$$

1.19. So we have:

$$x^2 + 4x + 3$$

There is nothing in front of the x^2 term so $a = 1$. The next step is to find p which is half of the number in front of x. So $p = 2$. So far we have:

$$(x + 2)^2 + q$$

When we multiply out $(x + 2)^2$ you get a $+4$ term. But you need a $+3$ at the end. Hence $q = -1$. Thus the equation is factorised as:

$$x^2 + 4x + 3 = (x + 2)^2 - 1$$

1.20. (a) 1.290 (b) 0.004490 (c) 7060

The key thing to remember is that zeros only count if they are between two significant figures. In (b) the first three zeros are not counted as significant figures but in (c) the first zero between 7 and 6 is counted.

1.21. So we have:

$$\frac{10000}{5 \times 10^6}$$

We need to convert the numerator to scientific notation. Notice that the power is just the number of zeros:

$$10000 = 1 \times 10^4$$

Hence:

$$\frac{10000}{5 \times 10^6} = \frac{1 \times 10^4}{5 \times 10^6}$$

We know that

$$\frac{1}{5} = 0.2$$

We also know that when dividing numbers with powers we subtract the powers. Hence we get:

$$\frac{1 \times 10^4}{5 \times 10^6} = 0.2 \times 10^{-2}$$

This is not scientific notation. We need to move everything to the left one so subtract one from the power to get the final answer:

$$2 \times 10^{-3}$$

1.22. The gradient is 0. If we move along in x we don't move up or down in y. Hence there is no gradient.

1.23. We can start by getting the angle of the apex of the triangle. Since we have a straight line the angles add up to $180°$. Hence we get the apex angle from:

$$180 - 113 = 67°$$

Since the triangle is isosceles, the remaining angles are equal and we know that the angles in a triangle add up to $180°$so we can get the remaining angles from:

$$\frac{180 - 67}{2} = 56.5°$$

Since C is the centre and A touches the circle the line AC is the radius of the circle and has a length of 5. If we draw a line vertically down from point C we get the right angled triangle (always check the angles add to $180°$):

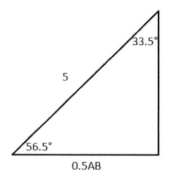

We can get $0.5AB$ using trigonometry like so:

$$cos(\theta) = \frac{adjacent}{hypotenuse}$$

$$cos(56.5) = \frac{0.5AB}{5}$$

$$0.5AB = 5 \times cos(56.5)$$

$$0.5AB = 2.76$$

Therefore:

$$AB = 5.52$$

8.2   Relationships

2.1. The formula for a line is given by:

$$y = mx + c$$

The question tells us that m=4 so:

$$y = 4x + c$$

We know from the point (8,35) that when x=8, y=35. So we can solve for c:

$$35 = 4(8) + c$$

$$35 = 32 + c$$

$$c = 35 - 32 = 3$$

Hence the equation of the line is:

$$y = 4x + 3$$

As a check you can put the information back in and ensure it fits together correctly:

$$35 = 4(8) + 3$$

$$35 = 35...correct$$

2.2. You can see that the line crosses the y-axis at $y = 3$. Hence $c = 3$. So:

$$y = mx + 3$$

The point (1,8) is on the line so we can solve for m (alternatively you can use the gradient formula):

$$8 = m + 3$$

$$m = 5$$

Hence the answer is:

$$y = 5x + 3$$

2.3. The second line intersects the w axis at $d-3$. Since the lines are parallel the gradients are equal so the gradient is q. Hence the equation is:

$$w = qv + d - 3$$

2.4. The starting point here is to find the equations of the two lines:

Line 1:
$$y = 2x + 5$$

Line 2:
$$y = 4x + 10$$

The lines will intercept when line 1 and line 2 have the same y value i.e. y=y. Thus we can say that:

$$2x + 5 = 4x + 10$$

Solve for x:

$$-2x = 5$$

$$x = -2.5$$

Put this back into one of the equations (say line 1) to find y:

$$y = 2x + 5 = 2(-2.5) + 5 = 0$$

Hence the two lines intersect at the point (-2.5,0).

2.5. These two lines are parallel and therefore they don't meet (technically they do meet at $x, y = \pm\infty$).

2.6. The gradient is one. It intersects with $y = -x$ at $(0, 0)$.

2.7. The equation tells us that the point (a,b) is on line Q and the point (a-4, b+1) is also on the line. If you drew a sketch this would be obvious. Hence we apply the gradient formula:

$$m = \frac{b + 1 - b}{a - 4 - a} = -\frac{1}{4}$$

If you have your eyes open you will see that as we move backwards 4 units in x (from a to $a - 4$) we move up one (from b to $b + 1$). Hence the gradient must be $-\frac{1}{4}$. Moving backwards makes the line go up so gradient must be negative and for every one unit you move in x you move $\pm\frac{1}{4}$ in y.

2.8. We know that $x = \frac{1}{2}(\pm\sqrt{17} - 5)$ is a solution. Hence we know that the two solutions are:

$$x = \frac{1}{2}(\sqrt{17} - 5) = 0$$

and

$$x = \frac{1}{2}(-\sqrt{17} - 5) = 0$$

Take these to the other side to get the two equations:

$$x - \frac{1}{2}(\sqrt{17} - 5) = 0$$

and

$$x - \frac{1}{2}(-\sqrt{17} - 5) = 0$$

These are our two factors. Hence we can factorise $x^2 + 5x + 2 = 0$ as:

$$(x - \frac{1}{2}(-\sqrt{17} - 5))(x - \frac{1}{2}(\sqrt{17} - 5)) = 0$$

2.9. There are two possible ways to answer this. Either find it or use the discriminant from the quadratic formula. When there is only one solution we know that:

$$b^2 - 4ac = 0*$$

A quadratic equation takes the form:

$$ax^2 + bx + c = 0$$

Comparing this with our equation $x^2 + 6x + 9 = 0$ gives a=1, b=6 and c=9. Substituting into equation * gives:

$$6^2 - 4(1)(9) = 36 - 36 = 0$$

Alternatively you could have found the only solution which is $x = -3$

2.10. A cube has volume l^3. All of the sites of the cube are length l. A face will have an area of $l \times l = l^2$. Hence any face, such as this one, would have area l^2:

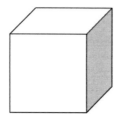

2.11. Depth d goes into the page and height runs up the page. Hence dh will be the shaded face:

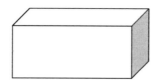

2.12. Take each one in turn and apply your knowledge of the discriminant $D = b^2 - 4ac$. If $D < 0$ we have no real roots if $D = 0$ we have one real and equal root and if $D > 0$ we have two real and distinct roots.

(1) This has only one root which is $x = 2$
(2) D=85 which is positive so we have two real and distinct roots
(3) D=-179 which is negative so we have no real roots

The final answer is therefore (2).

2.13. From reading the question the second equation is:

$$1729 = 9^3 + x^3$$

Solve for x:

$$1729 - 729 = x^3$$

$$x^3 = 1000$$

$$x = 10$$

2.14. The equation is hideous:

$$R = \frac{2(x-3)^4 + \sqrt{2}^2(x-3)^2}{(x-3)^2}$$

We should tidy it up. Obviously $\sqrt{2}^2 = 2$, so:

$$R = \frac{2(x-3)^4 + 2(x-3)^2}{(x-3)^2}$$

Now factorise using the common factor of $(x-3)^2$:

$$R = \frac{(x-3)^2(2(x-3)^2 + 2)}{(x-3)^2}$$

Obviously this cancels leaving:

$$R = 2(x-3)^2 + 2$$

To plot this we need a table for x and R between $x = 0$ and $x = 6$.

x	0	1	2	3	4	5	6
R	20	10	4	2	4	10	20

When you plot this you will get a graph which looks like this. If you do not simplify and just put x into the first equation; you will get the wrong answer (e.g. you will think that $R = \infty$ at $x = 3$ which is wrong).

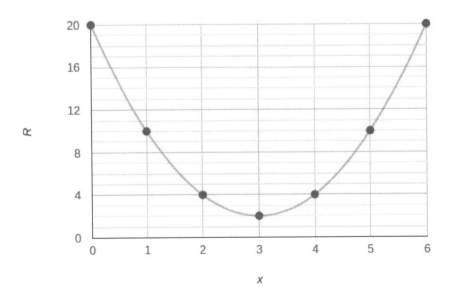

2.15. The equation of a parabola is of the form:

$$y = k(x - a)^2 + b$$

The turning point is at (a,b) and the axis of symmetry is at $x = a$. In this case we have the equation:

$$y = -2(x + 1)^2 + 4$$

The turning point is (-1,4) and the axis of symmetry is $x = -1$. The parabola has a maximum turning point due to the minus (it is upside down so the turning point is at the highest point so we call it a maximum).

2.16. The equation (when multiplied out) will have x^2 as its highest power term so we expect a parabola. The lowest value of y will occur at the turning point for a minimum turning point (i.e. a happy face). However the form of the equation doesn't look right... We need to write in a form we understand. The first step is to multiply out the equation:

$$y = (x - 1)(x - 2) - 3 = x^2 - 3x - 1$$

Now complete the square which gives:

$$y = (x - \frac{3}{2})^2 - \frac{13}{4}$$

Hence the turning point is $(\frac{3}{2}, -\frac{13}{4})$. Therefore the lowest value of y is $y = -\frac{13}{4}$ which occurs at the point where $x = \frac{3}{2}$

2.17. The equation of this parabola is:

$$y = -(x - 1)^2 - 2$$

The negative comes from the fact that the turning point is a maximum. The parabola when graphed looks as so:

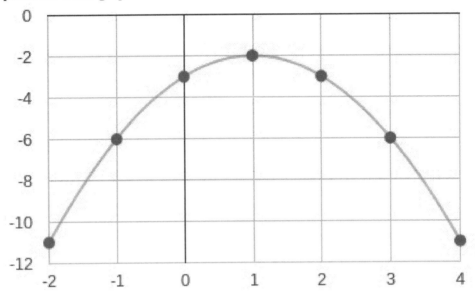

2.18. The two turning points are (2,1) and (5,5). These are connected by line P. A basic sketch of the geometry - not to scale- is given by:

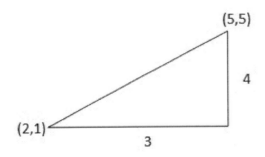

From Pythagoras we can say that:

$$P = \sqrt{(3^2 + 4^2)}$$

Therefore the length of P is:

$$P = 5$$

2.19. The first step is to eliminate one of the variables.

$$4x + 5y = 19 - - - Eqn1$$

$$2x + 3y = 9 - - - Eqn2$$

Let's get rid of y. So multiply eqn 1 by 3 and eqn 2 by 5. Hence:

$$12x + 15y = 57 - - - Eqn1(\times 3)$$

$$10x + 15y = 45 - - - Eqn2(\times 5)$$

Subtract the two equations:

$$2x = 12$$

$$x = 6$$

Then substitute x in eqn 1 and solve for y:

$$4(6) + 5y = 19$$

$$5y = 19 - 24$$

$$5y = -5$$

$$y = -1$$

Check that this is correct by substituting x and y into the other equation (eqn 2).

$$2(6) + 3(-1) = 9....Correct!$$

2.20. The first step is to write an equation for the relationship. Let a bat cost x and a ball cost y. Hence:

$$x + y = 1.10$$
$$x - y = 1$$

Add the two equations:

$$2x = 2.10$$
$$x = 1.05$$

Substitute into the first equation:

$$1.05 + y = 1.10$$
$$y = 0.05$$

So a ball costs £0.05p and a bat costs £1.05. You can check this in the other equation:

$$1.05 - 0.05 = 1...correct$$

2.21. Just follow the basic algebra. It's long but you know all the rules.

$$T' = T\sqrt{1 - \frac{V^2}{c^2}}$$

$$\frac{T'}{T} = \sqrt{1 - \frac{V^2}{c^2}}$$

$$\left(\frac{T'}{T}\right)^2 = 1 - \frac{V^2}{c^2}$$

$$\left(\frac{T'}{T}\right)^2 - 1 = -\frac{V^2}{c^2}$$

$$1 - \left(\frac{T'}{T}\right)^2 = \frac{V^2}{c^2}$$

$$c^2\left(1 - \left(\frac{T'}{T}\right)^2\right) = v^2$$

$$\sqrt{c^2\left(1 - \left(\frac{T'}{T}\right)^2\right)} = v$$

We can tidy this up a little:

$$v = \sqrt{c^2}\sqrt{1 - \left(\frac{T'}{T}\right)^2}$$

$$v = c\sqrt{1 - \left(\frac{T'}{T}\right)^2}$$

2.22. The hypotenuse is the longest side. $\sqrt{5} \approx 2.24$ so the right angle is expected to be opposite the side labeled $\sqrt{5}x$. We prove that there is a right angle with the converse of Pythagoras. If there is a right angle:

$$c^2 = a^2 + b^2$$

So check if this is the case:

$$\left(\sqrt{5}x\right)^2 = (2x)^2 + x^2$$

$$5x^2 = 4x^2 + x^2$$

$$5x^2 = 5x^2$$

Hence the triangle must have a right angle.

2.23. There are various ways to get the right answer. The simplest is to look at the value of y at $x = 0$ which on the graph is 1. We know that $sin(0) = 0$. So we want $y = 0$ at $x = 0$. We can do this by moving the graph forward by 90 degrees. Therefore a cosine graph is just a sine graph moved 90 degrees. Hence we get the answer:

$$y = cos(x) = sin(x + 90)$$

2.24. So we have the inequality:

$$-4x < -8$$

We need to divide through by -4. Remember that when we divide by a negative number we switch the inequality sign. Hence the answer:

$$x > 2$$

2.25. The first step is to rearrange the equations to get something that is easy to plot. Doing this gives:

$$E = 4x + 3$$

$$E = 5x + 1$$

All you need to do now is draw a graph of the two equations and find the point that the lines meet:

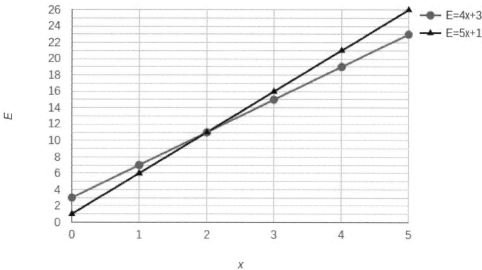

Hence the solution is $E = 11$ and $x = 2$.

8.3 Applications

3.1. (a) When adding fractions you need a common denominator (i.e. the same number on the bottom of both fractions). When you have this you just add the numerators (the number on top) together. To get a common denominator multiply the top and bottom of each fraction by the opposite denominator. So:

$$\frac{1}{2} + \frac{1}{4} = \frac{1}{2} \times \frac{4}{4} + \frac{1}{4} \times \frac{2}{2} = \frac{4}{8} + \frac{2}{8} = \frac{6}{8} = \frac{6 \div 2}{8 \div 2} = \frac{3}{4}$$

The above method works 100 % of the time. Alternatively you can simply do:

$$\frac{1}{2} + \frac{1}{4} = \frac{2}{4} + \frac{1}{4} = \frac{3}{4}$$

(b) Subtracting fractions works exactly the same way as adding fractions. So:

$$\frac{3}{5} - \frac{80}{400} = \frac{1200}{2000} - \frac{400}{2000} = \frac{800}{2000} = \frac{800 \div 100}{2000 \div 100} = \frac{8}{20} = \frac{8 \div 4}{20 \div 4} = \frac{2}{5}$$

(c) Same again but pay attention to the minus sign:

$$-\frac{5}{2} + \frac{3}{4} = -\frac{20}{8} + \frac{6}{8} = -\frac{14}{8} = -\frac{7}{4}$$

(d) When multiplying fractions just multiply the tops and bottoms together:

$$\frac{1}{2} \times \frac{1}{2} = \frac{1}{4}$$

(e) Notice that $2 \div 1$ is 2. So:

$$2 + \frac{7}{19} = \frac{2}{1} + \frac{7}{19} = \frac{38}{19} + \frac{7}{19} = \frac{45}{19}$$

(f) Do the multiplication first:

$$\frac{6}{7} + 2 \times \frac{0.5}{7} = \frac{6}{7} + \frac{1}{7} = \frac{7}{7} = 1$$

(g) Start by re-writing the decimal as a fraction:

$$0.7 + \frac{2}{20} = \frac{7}{10} + \frac{2}{20} = \frac{14}{20} + \frac{2}{20} = \frac{16}{20} = \frac{4}{5}$$

(h) Remember BODMAS so do brackets first.

$$\left(\frac{1}{5} + \frac{1}{4}\right) \div \frac{5}{4} = \frac{9}{20} \div \frac{5}{4} = \frac{9}{20} \times \frac{4}{5} = \frac{36}{100} = \frac{9}{25}$$

(i) Remember BODMAS. Brackets first, then divide then add.

$$\left(\frac{1}{2}\right)^2 + \frac{1}{y} \div \frac{1}{x} = \left(\frac{1}{2} \times \frac{1}{2}\right) + \frac{1}{y} \div \frac{1}{x} = \frac{1}{4} + \frac{1}{y} \div \frac{1}{x} = \frac{1}{4} + \frac{x}{y} = \frac{y + 4x}{4y}$$

3.2. Start with the top:

$$\frac{1}{x} + \frac{1}{y} = \frac{y + x}{xy}$$

Then the bottom:

$$\frac{1}{y} - z = \frac{1}{y} - \frac{z}{1} = \frac{1 - zy}{y}$$

Put it back together:

$$\frac{\frac{y+x}{xy}}{\frac{1-zy}{y}}$$

This is the same as:

$$\frac{y + x}{xy} \div \frac{1 - zy}{y} = \frac{y + x}{xy} \times \frac{y}{1 - zy} = \frac{y(y + x)}{xy(1 - zy)} = \frac{(y + x)}{x(1 - zy)}$$

3.3. Start by using your calculator or knowledge to find that $sin(45) = \frac{1}{\sqrt{2}}$.

$$\frac{5}{2} \times \frac{1}{sin(45)} = \frac{5}{2} \times \frac{1}{\frac{1}{\sqrt{2}}} = \frac{5}{2} \times \left(1 \div \frac{1}{\sqrt{2}}\right) = \frac{5}{2} \times \frac{1}{1} \times \frac{\sqrt{2}}{1} = \frac{5}{2} \times \sqrt{2} = \frac{5\sqrt{2}}{2}$$

3.4. 1.5% as a decimal is 0.015. If we say the cost of the house is P we can say that:

$$0.015P = 3840$$

Hence divide both sides by 0.015 so:

$$P = \frac{3840}{0.015} = 256,000$$

So the house cost £256,000. We can be sure this is correct because if we take the cost of the house and times this by the commission rate we should get back the fee which we do:

$$256000 \times 0.015 = 3840$$

3.5. We need to use the compound growth formula:

$$V_{final} = V_{initial} \times growth^{years}$$

$$V_{final} = 1000 \times 1.208^{2015-1965}$$

$$V_{final} = 12686642.9$$

Or approximately £12.7M which rounds to £13M.

3.6. (i) A ball thrown in the air is going in the z direction. The components of a vector are:

$$\begin{pmatrix} x \\ y \\ z \end{pmatrix}$$

In the case of a ball thrown up by x in the z direction we get the vector:

$$\begin{pmatrix} 0 \\ 0 \\ x \end{pmatrix}$$

(ii) The magnitude of the vector is:

$$\sqrt{0^2 + 0^2 + x^2} = x$$

Hence the unit position vector is:

$$\begin{pmatrix} 0 \\ 0 \\ 1 \end{pmatrix}$$

3.7. (i) If the two magnitudes are equal we can say that:

$$\sqrt{x^2 + x^2 + x^2} = \sqrt{3^2 + 0^2 + 3^2}$$

$$\sqrt{3x^2} = \sqrt{18}$$

$$\sqrt{3}x = \sqrt{9 \times 2}$$

$$\sqrt{3}x = 3\sqrt{2}$$

Solving for x:

$$x = \frac{3\sqrt{2}}{\sqrt{3}}$$

Get a rational denominator:

$$x = \frac{3\sqrt{2}\sqrt{3}}{3}$$

Cancel the 3 and combine the square roots:

$$x = \sqrt{6}$$

Note that $x = -\sqrt{6}$ is also a solution. But clearly a vector cannot have a negative length!

(ii) Start by finding $2B$:

$$2B = 2\begin{pmatrix} 3 \\ 0 \\ 3 \end{pmatrix} = \begin{pmatrix} 2 \times 3 \\ 2 \times 0 \\ 3 \times 2 \end{pmatrix} = \begin{pmatrix} 6 \\ 0 \\ 6 \end{pmatrix}$$

Therefore:

$$C = A + 2B = \begin{pmatrix} x \\ x \\ x \end{pmatrix} + \begin{pmatrix} 6 \\ 0 \\ 6 \end{pmatrix} = \begin{pmatrix} x + 6 \\ 0 \\ x + 6 \end{pmatrix}$$

(iii) Start by defining A and $-A$:

$$A = \begin{pmatrix} x \\ x \\ x \end{pmatrix}$$

$$-A = \begin{pmatrix} -x \\ -x \\ -x \end{pmatrix}$$

Calculate the magnitude of vector A:

$$\sqrt{x^2 + x^2 + x^2} = \sqrt{3x^2}$$

Now vector -A:

$$\sqrt{(-x)^2 + (-x)^2 + (-x)^2} = \sqrt{3x^2}$$

These are equal as expected.

3.8. Start by calculating the average. Sum the ages then divide by the number of players to find the mean, $\overline{X}$

$$\overline{X} = \frac{3 \times 6 + 2 \times 7 + 8 + 122}{7} = 23.14$$

Hence we can say that the average player in the team is 23 years old. This is silly. The average does not represent the sample at all. If you picked a player at random the average could be more than treble their age or almost 100 years off. The standard deviation, σ quantifies how good an average is. The formula for standard deviation is:

$$\sigma = \sqrt{\frac{\sum (X - \overline{X})^2}{N - 1}}$$

Let's start with the summation $\sum (X - \overline{X})^2$. This just means find the difference between every data point and the mean then add these differences up and square it. We can do this in a table:

Standard Deviation			
Data X	Mean $\overline{X}$	$X - \overline{X}$	$(X - \overline{X})^2$
6	23.14	-17.14	293.78
6	23.14	-17.14	293.78
6	23.14	-17.14	293.78
7	23.14	-16.14	260.50
7	23.14	-16.14	260.50
8	23.14	-15.14	229.22
122	23.14	98.86	9973.30
		N	7
		$\sum (X - \overline{X})^2$	11404.86

If we substitute these values into the equation we get:

$$\sigma = \sqrt{\frac{\sum (X - \overline{X})^2}{N - 1}} = \sqrt{\frac{11404.86}{7 - 1}} = 43.6$$

This standard deviation is stupidly big which tells you that the average is nonsense.

3.9. So we have the definitions:

$$tan\theta = \frac{sin\theta}{cos\theta}$$

$$cot\theta = 1 \div tan\theta$$

We can substitute for $tan\theta$:

$$cot\theta = 1 \div \frac{sin\theta}{cos\theta}$$

Using basic rules:

$$cot\theta = \frac{1}{1} \times \frac{cos\theta}{sin\theta}$$

Hence:

$$cot\theta = \frac{cos\theta}{sin\theta}$$

3.10. Think in terms of rows and this is very easy:

$$2\begin{pmatrix} 1 \\ 3 \\ 6 \end{pmatrix} + \begin{pmatrix} 4 \\ 2 \\ 1 \end{pmatrix} = \begin{pmatrix} 2 \\ 6 \\ 12 \end{pmatrix} + \begin{pmatrix} 4 \\ 2 \\ 1 \end{pmatrix} = \begin{pmatrix} 6 \\ 8 \\ 13 \end{pmatrix}$$

3.11. Start with the Pythagoras theorem and remember that side c is the hypotenuse.

$$c^2 = a^2 + b^2$$

Substitute for what we are given:

$$\left(\frac{1}{x}\right)^2 = \left(\frac{1}{3x}\right)^2 + S^2$$

Multiply out the brackets:

$$\frac{1}{x^2} = \frac{1}{9x^2} + S^2$$

Rearrange for S:

$$S^2 = \frac{1}{x^2} - \frac{1}{9x^2}$$

Combine fractions:

$$S^2 = \frac{8}{9x^2}$$

Square root both sides:

$$S = \sqrt{\frac{8}{9x^2}}$$

Optionally (though not really much of a simplification) this can be written as:

$$S = \frac{2\sqrt{2}}{3x}$$

We can check to make sure we have not made any mistakes by putting the final answer back into Pythagoras:

$$\left(\frac{1}{x}\right)^2 = \left(\frac{1}{3x}\right)^2 + \left(\sqrt{\frac{8}{9x^2}}\right)^2$$

$$\left(\frac{1}{x^2}\right) = \left(\frac{1}{9x^2}\right) + \left(\frac{8}{9x^2}\right) = \left(\frac{9}{9x^2}\right)$$

3.12. The first step is to write our data in order from the lowest to the highest:

1, 1, 2, 2, 2, 4, 4, 4, 4, 5, 5, 5, 6, 7, 7, 8, 8, 9, 16

There are 19 numbers so $n = 19$. The median for odd data is the $\frac{n+1}{2}$ number. So the median is the 10th number which is 5. Now look at the data before and after the median:

1st half: 1,1,2,2,2,4,4,4,4
2nd half: 5,5,6,7,7,8,8,9,16

Find the median again. For the first half it is 2 and for the second half it is 7. Hence $Q_{lower} = 2$ and $Q_{upper} = 7$. The interquartile range is the difference between the upper and lower quartiles - so 5. The semi-interquartile range is half of this so 2.5.

3.13. The simplest way to solve the problem is to use the sine rule. The sine rule states that:

$$\frac{a}{sin(A)} = \frac{b}{sin(B)} = \frac{c}{sin(C)}$$

We have both terms in b and one out of two of those in a. Hence we can solve for angle A:

$$\frac{a}{sin(A)} = \frac{b}{sin(B)}$$

$$\frac{54}{sin(A)} = \frac{100}{sin(47)}$$

$$\frac{54}{sin(A)} = 136.73$$

$$\frac{54}{136.73} = sin(A)$$

$$sin(A) = 0.395$$

$$A = sin^{-1}(0.395)$$

$$A = 23.3°$$

The angles of a triangle must add up to 180° so angle C must be:

$$C = 180 - 47 - 23.3 = 109.7°$$

3.14. (π). Start by labeling the sides:

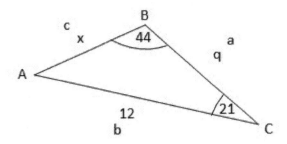

Now use the sine rule to calculate x:

$$\frac{b}{sin(B)} = \frac{c}{sin(C)}$$

$$\frac{12}{sin(44)} = \frac{x}{sin(21)}$$

$$x = 6.19$$

We then use the cosine rule to find q. We want side a so we use:

$$a^2 = b^2 + c^2 - 2bccos(A)$$

However we don't have angle A. But we can get it from:

$$A = 180 - 44 - 21 = 115°$$

Hence the cosine rule becomes:

$$a^2 = 12^2 + 6.19^2 - 2(12)(6.19)cos(115)$$

$$a^2 = 245.1$$

$$a = 15.66$$

3.15. The area of a triangle is calculated from the formula:

$$Area = \frac{1}{2}absin(C)$$

Hence:

$$Area = \frac{1}{2} \times 15.66 \times 12 \times sin(21)$$

$$Area = 33.67$$

8.4   Practice Problems Set 1

4.1. So we have the inequality:

$$10 < x + 5$$

We first need to subtract 5 from both sides:

$$5 < x$$

When we flip an equation we flip the sign. Hence:

$$x > 5$$

Do a common sense check using the equation in the question. If $x = 4$ we get $10 < 9$ from the first equation which is nonsense. If $x = 5$ we get $10 < 10$ which is also nonsense. However if x=6 (i.e. $x > 5$) we get $10 < 11$ which makes sense.

4.2. So we have a squared term and a non-square term:

$$(x - 2)^2(x + 1)$$

We start with the square term:

$$(x - 2)^2 = (x - 2)(x - 2) = x^2 - 4x + 4$$

Hence we now need:

$$(x^2 - 4x + 4)(x + 1) = x^3 - 3x^2 + 4$$

4.3. The two key rules needed here are 1) when you bring a power to the top it becomes negative and 2) when you multiply you add the powers. Hence:

$$\frac{x^{y+2}}{x^{y^2+2y-8}} = x^{y+2} \times x^{-y^2-2y+8} = x^{-y^2-y+10}$$

4.4. Start with the mean:

$$\overline{X} = \frac{3 + 6 + 7 + 2 + 8 + 9 + 5 + 8}{8} = 6$$

Now we need the standard deviation which we get from:

$$\sigma = \sqrt{\frac{\sum (X - \overline{X})^2}{N - 1}}$$

Now create a table:

Standard Deviation			
Data X	Mean $\overline{X}$	$X - \overline{X}$	$\left(X - \overline{X}\right)^2$
3	6	-3	9
6	6	0	0
7	6	1	1
2	6	-4	16
8	6	2	4
9	6	3	9
5	6	-1	1
8	6	1	4
		N	8
		$\sum \left(X - \overline{X}\right)^2$	44

We can now get the standard deviation from:

$$\sigma = \sqrt{\frac{\sum \left(X - \overline{X}\right)^2}{N - 1}} = \sqrt{\frac{44}{8 - 1}} = 2.507$$

Putting the mean and standard deviation together in the form asked for in the question gives the final answer:

$$6 \pm 2.5$$

4.5. The first experiment has a result of 6 ± 2.5 so the highest value it could be is 8.5 and the lowest is 3.5. For the second experiment which has a result of 9 ± 0.4 we have an answer between 9.4 and 8.6. There is no overlap. Hence the scientist is wrong.

The second experiment has a much lower standard deviation so is expected to be more reliable i.e. there is much less variation between readings on average.

4.6. The equation is $x = a$.

4.7. Start by finding the gradient of the line.

$$m = \frac{q-3}{3-1} = \frac{q-3}{2}$$

The equation of a line is given by:

$$y - b = m(x - a)$$

Hence:

$$y - 3 = \frac{q-3}{2}(x-1)$$

$$y = \frac{q-3}{2}(x-1) + 3$$

$$y = \frac{q-3}{2}x - \frac{9-q}{2}$$

4.8. We can easily find k by looking at the graph. The highest point is 3 and the lowest is -3. Hence $k = 3$.

For a sine graph we expect it to be 0° at 180°, however it is zero at 150°. We need to move it forward 30°- so $\phi_1 = 30$. For a cosine graph (which has not been shifted up or down) we expect it to be at a maximum at 0° but this maximum occurs at 60°. So we need to move the graph backwards 60 degrees so $\phi_2 = -60$. Hence:

$$y = k sin(x + 30)$$

Or

$$y = k cos(x - 60)$$

You can check you have the right answer by ensuring that $y = y$. For example at $x = 60°$ we can see that:

$$y = 3sin(90) = 3cos(0) = 3$$

4.9. If you lose 91% you are left with 9% and 9% as a decimal is 0.09. Hence we can get the original value from:

$$\frac{1170}{0.09} = 13,000$$

So the investor originally put in £13,000.

4.10. Start by counting the number of places to the right the first number is (including the zero before the decimal point). It is seven. Hence:

$$0.0000003 = 3 \times 10^{-7}$$

4.11. First move the graph 90 degrees then double all of the points. Hence you get:

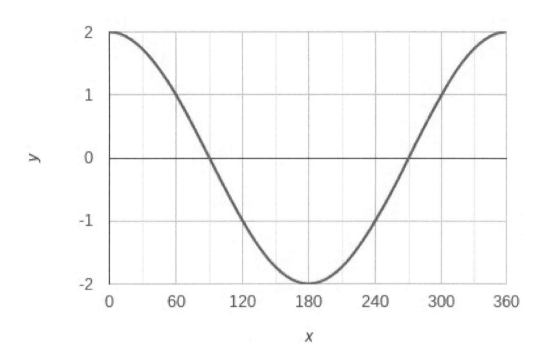

4.12. We need to write out the two equations:

$$2A + 5P = 1.90$$

$$A + 4P + B = 1.80$$

We know that B=£0.4. Hence:

$$2A + 5P = 1.90$$

$$A + 4P = 1.40$$

Multiply the second equation by two and subtract:

$$3P = 0.90$$

$$P = 0.30$$

Now solve for A:

$$A + 4(0.3) = 1.40$$

$$A = 0.2$$

Lastly check the answer in the first equation to make sure that it is right:

$$2(0.2) + 5(0.3) = 1.90...correct$$

4.13. In decimal terms prices moved up 1.21 times. Hence we just divide by this:

$$\frac{650}{1.21} = 537.19$$

Hence they paid £537.19 last year.

4.14. Start by doing the multiplication and subtraction:

$$4A - 0.5B = \begin{pmatrix} 7 \\ 9 \\ 16 \end{pmatrix}$$

Now find the magnitude:

$$\sqrt{7^2 + 9^2 + 16^2} = 19.65$$

4.15. Start by calculating the volume of the cylinder

$$V = \pi R^2 h = \pi \times 1.5^2 \times 4 = 28.27 m^3$$

Now find 78% of this:

$$V_{water} = 0.78 \times 28.27 = 22.05 m^3$$

4.16. Notice that we can divide though by 3 (or take a common factor and cancel by dividing both sides by 3). Either way we can get rid of the 3.

$$3x^2 + 3x - 6 = x^2 + x - 2 = 0$$

Now it's easy to factorise:

$$x^2 + x - 2 = (x + 2)(x - 1) = 0$$

Hence the solutions are $x = -2$ and $x = 1$.

4.17. The key is to rearrange the equation to get t on one side:

$$\frac{t}{4} + \frac{15}{8} = 4t$$

$$\frac{15}{8} = 4t - \frac{t}{4}$$

$$\frac{15}{8} = \frac{15t}{4}$$

Times both sides by 4:

$$\frac{60}{8} = 15t$$

Flip:

$$15t = \frac{60}{8}$$

Divide both sides by 15:

$$t = \frac{60}{120}$$

Simplify:

$$t = \frac{1}{2}$$

8.5   Practice Problems Set 2

5.1. Start by putting it in your calculator:

$$\frac{\pi}{272} = 0.011549973...$$

We need four significant figures and we don't count the first zeros. Leading zeros are not significant. Hence the answer is 0.01155.

5.2. The equation we have does not look right:

$$y + 15 = 4x + 18 - 2$$

There are two methods we could use. The simplest is to rearrange the equation to the following by subtracting 15 from both sides:

$$y = 4x + 1$$

Note that:

$$y = mx + c$$

Clearly from comparing the equations the gradient is 4 and the y intercept is 1.

Alternatively, we can simplify to:

$$y + 15 = 4x + 16$$

Which we can factorise to:

$$y + 15 = 4(x + 4)$$

This matches with our equation:

$$y - b = m(x - a)$$

So $m = 4$ by comparing the equations. The y intercept occurs when $x = 0$. So at $x = 0$ the equation becomes:

$$y + 15 = 16$$

$$y = 1$$

Hence the y-intercept is 1.

5.3. It is just basic algebra.

$$T = 2\pi\sqrt{\frac{L}{g}}$$

$$\frac{T}{2\pi} = \sqrt{\frac{L}{g}}$$

$$\frac{T^2}{4\pi^2} = \frac{L}{g}$$

$$T^2 g = 4\pi^2 L$$

$$g = \frac{4\pi^2 L}{T^2}$$

5.4. Let's complete the square:

$$y = x^2 + 4x + 8 = (x + 2)^2 + 4$$

Hence the turning point is $(-2, 4)$

5.5. First step is to find kq. From what is given in the question we can say that:

$$kq = q^{-\frac{1}{2}}q = q^{\frac{1}{2}} = \sqrt{q} = \sqrt{16} = 4$$

Now we need to label the sides as so:

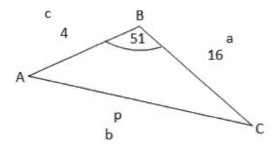

Now apply the cosine rule for side p:

$$b^2 = a^2 + c^2 - 2ac\cos(B)$$

$$p^2 = 16^2 + 4^2 - 2 \times 16 \times 4 \times \cos(51)$$

$$p^2 = 191.447$$

$$p = 13.84$$

5.6. If they lost 63% they are left with 37%. Hence we do:

$$\frac{3890.92}{0.37} = 10516$$

Therefore the investor invested £10,516.

5.7. Start with the multiplication then do the brackets and lastly do the division.

$$(2 \times \frac{2}{8} - \frac{1}{6}) \div \frac{2}{4}$$

$$= (\frac{4}{8} - \frac{1}{6}) \div \frac{2}{4}$$

$$= \frac{1}{3} \div \frac{2}{4}$$

$$= \frac{1}{3} \times \frac{4}{2}$$

$$= \frac{1}{3} \times 2$$

$$= \frac{2}{3}$$

5.8. This looks horrible but the answer is amazingly simple. Just work systematically and it is not hard. It's just multiplying out brackets twice.

$$\left(x - \left(\frac{5}{4} + \frac{\sqrt{89}}{4}\right)\right)\left(x + \left(\frac{\sqrt{89}}{4} - \frac{5}{4}\right)\right)$$

$$x^2 - \left(\frac{5}{4} + \frac{\sqrt{89}}{4}\right)x + \left(\frac{\sqrt{89}}{4} - \frac{5}{4}\right)x - \left(\frac{5}{4} + \frac{\sqrt{89}}{4}\right)\left(\frac{\sqrt{89}}{4} - \frac{5}{4}\right)*$$

Look at the middle terms (i.e. those multiplied by x):

$$-\left(\frac{5}{4} + \frac{\sqrt{89}}{4}\right)x + \left(\frac{\sqrt{89}}{4} - \frac{5}{4}\right)x$$

$$-\frac{5}{4}x - \frac{\sqrt{89}}{4}x + \frac{\sqrt{89}}{4}x - \frac{5}{4}x$$

$$-\frac{10}{4}x$$

Now multiply out the other bracket:

$$\left(\frac{5}{4} + \frac{\sqrt{89}}{4}\right)\left(\frac{\sqrt{89}}{4} - \frac{5}{4}\right)$$

$$\frac{5\sqrt{89}}{16} - \frac{25}{16} + \frac{89}{16} - \frac{5\sqrt{89}}{16}$$

The two $\frac{5\sqrt{89}}{16}$ cancel out which leaves:

$$-\frac{25}{16} + \frac{89}{16} = 4$$

Hence we get the answer (careful with signs - look closely at equation * to see why we have -4):

$$x^2 - \frac{10}{4}x - 4 = 0$$

Since the equation equals zero we can tidy it up by multiplying through by 2:

$$2x^2 - 5x - 8 = 0$$

5.9. Find coefficients a, b and c:

$$ax^2 + bx + c = 0$$

$$x^2 + 9x - 2 = 0$$

Hence $a = 1$, $b = 9$ and $c = -2$. Now use the discriminant:

$$b^2 - 4ac = 9^2 - 4(1)(-2) = 89$$

Therefore the equation has two real and distinct roots.

5.10. The money is invested for 52 years. It grows at 15% which is 1.15 as a decimal. Hence we can get the final value from:

$$10000 \times 1.15^{52} = 14331370$$

Or in other words £14.3 million pounds. Get saving - compound interest is incredible.

5.11. First step is to find two points on the line. We can spot the points (2.5,9) and (6,18). These are close enough for an estimate. Now we just use these points to find the equation of the line as normal:

$$m = \frac{18 - 9}{6 - 2.5} = 2.57$$

Now we need the y-intercept.

$$W = mV + c$$

$$18 = 2.57(6) + c$$

$$c = 2.58$$

Hence the equation is approximately:

$$W = 2.57V + 2.58$$

The computer generated solution is very close to our estimate:

$$W = 2.571V + 2.5$$

5.12. If you are paying attention you'll spot that this is a 3-4-5 triangle so clearly will have a right angle. However we must use the converse of Pythagoras. If the triangle has a right angle it must be the case that:

$$c^2 = a^2 + b^2$$

So let's check:

$$5^2 = 3^2 + 4^2$$

$$25 = 9 + 16$$

$$25 = 25$$

Hence the triangle has a right angle.

5.13. Start with the basics:

$$\frac{9}{\sqrt{27}} = \frac{9}{\sqrt{27}} \times \frac{\sqrt{27}}{\sqrt{27}} = \frac{9\sqrt{27}}{27}$$

If you are switched on you will be able to simplify this a lot:

$$\frac{9\sqrt{9} \times \sqrt{3}}{27} = \frac{27 \times \sqrt{3}}{27} = \frac{\sqrt{3}}{1} = \sqrt{3}$$

Hence $a = 3$.

5.14. (i) Start with the mean:

$$\overline{x} = \frac{6 + 4 + 8 + 4 + 6 + 8 + 12 + 2 + 4}{9} = 6$$

Now make up a table:

Standard Deviation			
Data X	Mean $\overline{X}$	$X - \overline{X}$	$(X - \overline{X})^2$
6	6	0	0
4	6	-2	4
8	6	2	4
4	6	-2	4
6	6	0	0
8	6	2	4
12	6	6	36
2	6	-4	16
4	6	-2	4
		N	9
		$\sum (X - \overline{X})^2$	72

Put this into the equation:

$$\sigma = \sqrt{\frac{\sum (X - \overline{X})^2}{N - 1}} = \sqrt{\frac{72}{9 - 1}} = 3$$

For the semi-interquartile range we need an ordered list:

2, 4, 4, 4, 6, 6, 8, 8, 12

So $Q_1 = 4$ and $Q_3 = 8$ so the interquartile range is 4 and hence the semi-interquartile range is 2.

(ii) On average the class scored the same but there was more variation in the test scores of the second class.

(iii) We would expect to see the third class have test scores more clustered around the average value than the test scores of the first class.

5.15. Screw factorising that thing - just use the quadratic formula. So get the coefficients:

$$ax^2 + bx + c = 0$$

$$4x^2 + 2x - 3 = 0$$

Therefore by comparing we can see that $a = 4$, $b = 2$ and $c = -3$

$$x = \frac{-b \pm \sqrt{b^2 - 4ac}}{2a}$$

$$x = \frac{-2 \pm \sqrt{2^2 - 4(4)(-3)}}{2(4)}$$

Hence:

$$x = -1.15$$

or

$$x = 0.65$$

Alternatively it is also correct to write your answer as:

$$x = -\frac{1}{4} \pm \frac{\sqrt{13}}{4}$$

5.16. Start by getting the equation. Notice that there are 5 complete cosine graphs so we expect a $5x$ term. The graph is between -4 and $+4$ so we expect to multiply by 4. As there is a maximum at $0°$ and $360°$ the graph has not been moved left or right so c is zero. Hence we get the equation:

$$y = 4cos(5x)$$

Thus $a = 4$, $b = 5$ and $c = 0$.

5.17. We will need the equation for the length of an arc and for the area of a sector.

$$A_{sector} = \pi R^2 \times \frac{\theta}{360}$$

$$L_{arc} = 2\pi R \times \frac{\theta}{360}$$

The question asks us to divide these two:

$$\frac{A_{sector}}{L_{arc}} = \left(\pi R^2 \times \frac{\theta}{360}\right) \div \left(2\pi R \times \frac{\theta}{360}\right) = \left(\pi R^2 \times \frac{\theta}{360}\right) \times \frac{1}{2\pi R \times \frac{\theta}{360}} = \frac{\pi R^2 \times \frac{\theta}{360}}{2\pi R \times \frac{\theta}{360}}$$

Lots of terms cancel:

$$\frac{\pi R^2 \times \frac{\theta}{360}}{2\pi R \times \frac{\theta}{360}} = \frac{R}{2}$$

This is an amazing and unexpectedly simple result. It is true - check it for yourself. Imagine you have a circle with radius of 10m and a sector with an angle of 60 degrees. The length of the arc is 10.47m and the area of the sector is $52.36m^2$. It all checks out:

$$\frac{52.36}{10.47} \approx 5$$

And:

$$\frac{R}{2} = \frac{10}{2} = 5$$

5.18. We need two points on the line to find its equation. We can find the points from the equation of the parabola. The line intercepts the parabola at $x = -2$ and $x = 3$. So find the y values at these points:

$$y = (x - 1)^2 + 1 = (-2 - 1)^2 + 1 = 10$$

$$y = (x - 1)^2 + 1 = (3 - 1)^2 + 1 = 5$$

So the points are $(-2, 10)$ and $(3, 5)$. From these two points we can calculate the equation of the line which comes to:

$$y = -x + 8$$

If you are switched on you will have spotted that the y axis scale goes up in 5's. At $x = 0$ the line looks to be about $y = 8$ which is what we expect from the equation. Hence the answer looks right.

8.6   Minimum Competency

6.1. The data is just 1,2,3,4. So let's start by finding the mean:

$$\bar{x} = \frac{1+2+3+4}{4} = 2.5$$

For the standard deviation make up a table like so:

Standard Deviation			
Data X	Mean $\overline{X}$	$X - \overline{X}$	$(X - \overline{X})^2$
1	2.5	-1.5	2.25
2	2.5	-0.5	0.25
3	2.5	0.5	0.25
4	2.5	1.5	2.25
		N	4
		$\sum (X - \overline{X})^2$	5

Put this into the equation:

$$\sigma = \sqrt{\frac{\sum (X - \overline{X})^2}{N - 1}} = \sqrt{\frac{5}{4 - 1}} = 1.29$$

6.2. Always start with the brackets:

$$\frac{2}{3} \div \frac{3}{4} = \frac{2}{3} \times \frac{4}{3} = \frac{8}{9}$$

Now do the addition (must get a common denominator):

$$\frac{8}{9} + \frac{1}{2} = \frac{8}{9} \times \frac{2}{2} + \frac{1}{2} \times \frac{9}{9} = \frac{16}{18} + \frac{9}{18} = \frac{25}{18}$$

6.3. Start by finding $\frac{1}{4}u$:

$$\frac{1}{4}u = \frac{1}{4}\begin{pmatrix} 8 \\ -16 \end{pmatrix} = \begin{pmatrix} 2 \\ -4 \end{pmatrix}$$

Now put it all together:

$$s = \frac{1}{4}u + v = \begin{pmatrix} 2 \\ -4 \end{pmatrix} + \begin{pmatrix} -9 \\ -6 \end{pmatrix} = \begin{pmatrix} -7 \\ -10 \end{pmatrix}$$

Now calculate the magnitude:

$$\sqrt{(-7)^2 + (-10)^2} = 12.21$$

6.4. First find the gradient with the formula and label the points $(2, 10) = (x_1, y_1)$ and $(5, 19) = (x_2, y_2)$.

$$m = \frac{y_2 - y_1}{x_2 - x_1} = \frac{19 - 10}{5 - 2} = \frac{9}{3} = 3$$

Now let $(2, 10) = (a, b)$ and use the formula:

$$y - b = m(x - a)$$

$$y - 10 = 3(x - 2)$$

$$y = 3x - 6 + 10$$

$$y = 3x + 4$$

You can check that this is correct by substituting back in:

$$y = 3(5) + 4 = 19...correct$$

6.5. We need to use the discriminant. The formula is:

$$b^2 - 4ac$$

We get a, b and c from comparing our equation with the standard form:

$$ax^2 + bx + c = 0$$

$$x^2 + 6x - 2 = 0$$

Therefore, $a = 1$, $b = 6$ and $c = -2$. Thus:

$$b^2 - 4ac = 6^2 - 4(1)(-2) = 36 + 8 = 44$$

Therefore we have two real and distinct roots

6.6. Just multiply everything in one bracket by everything in the other:

$$(x + 2)(x + 5) = x^2 + 5x + 2x + 10 = x^2 + 7x + 10$$

6.7. The parabola will have the turning point (-2,-5)

6.8. The turning point is at the bottom so it must be a minimum turning point.

6.9. So are given the equation below and we need to complete the square:

$$x^2 - 6x + 15 = 0$$

First step is to divide the middle number by two and that gives us $a = 3$.

$$(x - 3)^2 + b = 0$$

But when we multiply out we will do -3×-3 which will add a 9 however we want it to end in a $+15$. Now we solve for b:

$$9 + b = 15$$

$$b = 6$$

Hence we get the answer:

$$(x - 3)^2 + 6 = 0$$

6.10. At first glance it's obviously a sine graph. There is one complete sine graph between 0° and 180° and another between 180° and 360°. So there are 2 sine graphs. Therefore we have a $2x$ term. Since the graph is between 1 and -1 there is no need to multiply sine by anything. Putting this together gives the answer:

$$y = sin(2x)$$

6.11. As always multiply top and bottom by the denominator:

$$\frac{3}{\sqrt{6}} = \frac{3 \times \sqrt{6}}{\sqrt{6} \times \sqrt{6}} = \frac{3\sqrt{6}}{6}$$

Now ask: can I make this any simpler? The answer is yes. Cancel the 3:

$$\frac{3\sqrt{6}}{6} = \frac{\sqrt{6}}{2}$$

6.12. Clearly there is a common factor of 3:

$$3x^2 + 3x - 60 = 3(x^2 + x - 20)$$

Now we need two numbers that add to 1 and multiply to give -20. Clearly -4 and +5 do this. Hence:

$$3(x^2 + x - 20) = 3(x - 4)(x + 5)$$

6.13. The formula for the volume of a cone is:

$$V = \frac{1}{3}\pi R^2 h$$

If we substitute what we know we get:

$$V = \frac{1}{3} \times \pi \times 4^2 \times 10 = 167.55cm^3$$

Now we need to round to two significant figures so we get $170cm^3$. This is an odd answer but it is what the question wants.

6.14. Just follow basic algebra rules systematically:

$$W = \frac{1}{2}m(v^2 - u^2)$$

$$2W = m(v^2 - u^2)$$

$$\frac{2W}{m} = v^2 - u^2$$

$$\frac{2W}{m} + u^2 = v^2$$

$$v = \sqrt{\frac{2W}{m} + u^2}$$

6.15. Just like in question 6.5; we need to get the value of a, b and c by comparing our quadratic equation with the standard form of a quadratic equation:

$$ax^2 + bx + c = 0$$

$$2x^2 + 3x - 2 = 0$$

Hence $a = 2$, $b = 3$ and $c = -2$. So we can now use the quadratic formula to solve:

$$x = \frac{-b \pm \sqrt{b^2 - 4ac}}{2a}$$

$$x = \frac{-3 \pm \sqrt{3^2 - 4(2)(-2)}}{2(2)}$$

$$x = \frac{-3 \pm \sqrt{25}}{4}$$

$$x = \frac{-3 \pm 5}{4}$$

Hence we get the two solutions which are $x = -2$ or $x = 0.5$

6.16. It's just basic algebra. Nothing weird:

$$cos^2x + sin^2x = 1$$

$$cos^2x = 1 - sin^2x$$

$$cosx = \sqrt{1 - sin^2x}$$

6.17. Start by labeling the triangle. Angles have a capital letter and the sides have a small letter.

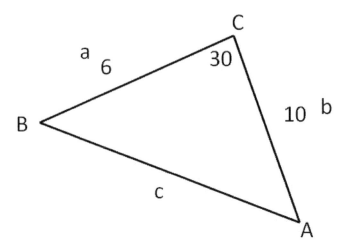

Now use the formula:

$$Area = \frac{1}{2}absin(C)$$

$$Area = \frac{1}{2} \times 6 \times 10 \times sin(30)$$

Those of you who know your stuff will know from memory that $sin(30) = \frac{1}{2}$. Hence:

$$Area = \frac{1}{4} \times 6 \times 10$$

$$Area = 15$$

If you watch the Big Bang Theory (specifically season 1, episode 2) you should know $sin(30) = \frac{1}{2}$

Leonard: "Okay! Now we've got an inclined plane. The force required to lift is reduced by the sine of the angle of the stairs, call it thirty degrees, so about half"

Sheldon: "Exactly half."

6.18. Just use the compound interest formula. Adding 0.25% is the same as multiplying by 1.0025. Hence do:

$$100 \times 1.0025^5 = 101.256$$

If we round this up we get the answer £101.26.

6.19. We first need to express 1000 in scientific notation:

$$1000 = 1 \times 10^3$$

Now we need to divide (so we subtract the powers):

$$\frac{10.9 \times 10^{12}}{1 \times 10^3}$$

Hence we get the answer:

$$10.9 \times 10^9 KWh$$

Which is, in words, 10.9 billion kilowatt hours.

6.20. When $x = 2$ we get an expression for g which is:

$$g = f(2) + 1$$

So we need $f(2)$. All we do here is substitute 2 for every x which gives:

$$f(2) = 2^2 + 2 + 1$$

$$f(2) = 7$$

Therefore:

$$g = f(2) + 1 = 7 + 1 = 8$$

8.7   Challenge Problems Set

In this section the answers will not show every single little step. By now you should be pretty good - the obvious will be omitted.

7.1. (i) The first part is easy:

$$\frac{\sqrt{m}}{n} = \frac{\sqrt{m}}{n} \times \frac{\sqrt{m}}{\sqrt{m}} = \frac{m}{n\sqrt{m}}$$

(ii) Clearly $m = 2$ and $n = 3$. Hence:

$$\frac{\sqrt{2}}{3} = \frac{2}{3\sqrt{2}}$$

(iii) Start by substituting $m = n$:

$$\frac{\sqrt{n}}{n} = \frac{n}{n\sqrt{n}}$$

$$\frac{\sqrt{n}}{n} = \frac{n}{n^{\frac{3}{2}}}$$

We can flip this to give the answer (i.e do one over both sides):

$$\frac{n}{\sqrt{n}} = \frac{n^{\frac{3}{2}}}{n}$$

This is of course correct. If you don't see why consider for example if:

$$\frac{1}{4} = \frac{1}{4}$$

Then:

$$\frac{4}{1} = \frac{4}{1}$$

(iv) Look at the denominator as that is all that matters:

$$n \times (\sqrt{n})^{2t+1} = n \times n^{t+\frac{1}{2}} = n^{t+\frac{3}{2}}$$

We can write this as:

$$n^{t+\frac{3}{2}} = n^{t+1+\frac{1}{2}}$$

Since you are always adding a half for all values of t the power will never be a whole number. Hence the denominator will never be rational.

7.2. Start with the zeros. These occur when the numerator is zero. Hence we solve:

$$s + 5 = 0$$

So:

$$s = -5$$

For the zeros we set the denominator equal to zero. Hence:

$$(s - 1)(s^2 + 3s + 2) = 0$$

Thus we have poles at s=1 and from the quadratic formula we get poles at s=-1 and s=-2.

(ii) Just basic fractions work:

$$\frac{1}{H(s)} = 1 \div H(s) = 1 \div \frac{(s + 5)}{(s - 1)(s^2 + 3s + 2)}$$

$$\frac{1}{H(s)} = \frac{(s - 1)(s^2 + 3s + 2)}{(s + 5)}$$

Hence the poles are the zeros and the zeros are the poles.

(iii) At a pole $H(s) = \infty$ hence the gradient must increase towards the pole.

7.3. Start with the magnitudes as they are easy:

$$|A| = \sqrt{13}$$

$$|B| = \sqrt{5}$$

Now the dot product, which you can figure out from the description, is:

$$A \cdot B = 2 \times 1 + 3 \times 2 = 8$$

Hence:

$$cos(\theta) = \frac{8}{\sqrt{13}\sqrt{5}}$$

$$\theta = 7.125°$$

Hence we have the length of two sides (the magnitudes) and the angle between them:

$$A = \frac{1}{2}absin(C) = \frac{1}{2} \times \sqrt{13} \times \sqrt{5} \times sin(7.125) = 0.5$$

7.4. It is not £10,000! Percentages are weird. The correct answer is:

$$(10000 \times 0.9^{10}) \times 1.1^{10} = 9043.82$$

So it is worth £9044 rounded to the nearest pound.

7.5. Clearly from the first equation we can see that $y = 1$ or $y = -1$. Thus we get two equations in x (one for $y = 1$ and one for $y = -1$):

$$x^2 - 2x + 1 = 0$$

And:

$$x^2 + 2x - 1 = 0$$

The first has solution $x = 1$ as it factorises to $(x - 1)^2 = 0$

The second has the solutions - from the quadratic formula - of $x = -1 \pm \sqrt{2}$.

7.6. Apply the quadratic formula. Hence you get the answer:

$$2(x + (\sqrt{2} - 1))(x - (1 + \sqrt{2})) = 0$$

7.7. (i) Use the quadratic formula:

$$x = \frac{-2\sqrt{a}\sqrt{c} \pm \sqrt{(2\sqrt{a}\sqrt{c})^2 - 4ac}}{2a}$$

$$x = \frac{-2\sqrt{a}\sqrt{c} \pm \sqrt{4ac - 4ac}}{2a}$$

$$x = \frac{-2\sqrt{a}\sqrt{c}}{2a}$$

$$x = -\frac{\sqrt{c}}{\sqrt{a}}$$

(ii) Clearly $a = 4$ and $c = 9$. Hence use the formula:

$$x = -\frac{\sqrt{9}}{\sqrt{4}} = -1.5$$

(iii) This question is just basic factorising. We know that:

$$\sqrt{c} \times \sqrt{c} = c$$

All of the terms are positive so there must be two plus terms. We can say that the answer will look like:

$$(qx + \sqrt{c})(qx + \sqrt{c}) = 0$$

We need to find q. So multiply out:

$$q^2 + 2q\sqrt{c} + c = 0$$

Therefore by comparing with the equation in 7.7(i) it's obvious that $q = \sqrt{a}$. So:

$$(\sqrt{a}x + \sqrt{c})(\sqrt{a}x + \sqrt{c}) = 0$$

$$(\sqrt{a}x + \sqrt{c})^2 = 0$$

Now let's rearrange to get the solution. First square both sides:

$$\sqrt{a}x + \sqrt{c} = 0$$

Hence:

$$x = -\frac{\sqrt{c}}{\sqrt{a}}$$

7.8. Look at the denominator:

$$\sqrt[3]{x} = x^{\frac{1}{3}}$$

We need the power of one. How do we get that?

$$x^1 = x^{\frac{1}{3}+\frac{2}{3}} = x^{\frac{1}{3}} \times x^{\frac{2}{3}}$$

Hence we can do:

$$\frac{y}{\sqrt[3]{x}} \times \frac{x^{\frac{2}{3}}}{x^{\frac{2}{3}}} = \frac{yx^{\frac{2}{3}}}{x} = \frac{y\sqrt[3]{x^2}}{x}$$

7.9. (i) Multiply out and compare terms:

$$x^2 + 81 = x^2 - 81q^2 = 0$$

So it must be true that:

$$81 = -81q^2$$

So solve for q:

$$1 = -q^2$$

$$q^2 = -1$$

$$q = \sqrt{-1}$$

If you solved this problem you are due congratulations on discovering complex numbers. You have just discovered the number i which is:

$$i = \sqrt{-1}$$

(ii) Just use the relevant part of the quadratic formula:

$$b^2 - 4ac = 0^2 - 4(1)(81) = -324$$

Since this is negative the equation has no real solutions.

(iii) Find the solution in terms of q:

$$(x - 9q) = 0$$

or

$$(x + 9q) = 0$$

Hence the two solutions are $\pm 9q$. Which if we substitute for q (which we found previously) means the two solutions are $\pm 9\sqrt{-1}$

7.10. The basic formulae when θ is in degrees are:

$$L = 2\pi R \times \frac{\theta}{360}$$

$$A = \pi R^2 \times \frac{\theta}{360}$$

We know that:

$$360° = 2\pi rad$$

Hence the equations in radians are:

$$L = R\theta$$

$$A = R^2 \times \frac{\theta}{2}$$

We can tidy up A:

$$A = \frac{1}{2}R^2\theta$$

With some jiggling we can substitute for L:

$$A = \frac{1}{2}R^2\theta = \frac{1}{2}R(R\theta)$$

Hence:

$$A = \frac{1}{2}R(R\theta) = \frac{1}{2}RL$$

19332911R00062

Printed in Great Britain
by Amazon